12/19/04

2 days after mom's
death   12/17/04 -
Thursday   5:25 AM

10/31/21

Wider Than the Sky

GERALD M. EDELMAN

Wider Than the Sky

the phenomenal gift of consciousness

yale university press   new haven and london

Designed by Sonia L. Shannon.
Set in Garamond type by
Achorn Graphic Services.
Printed in the United States of America by
R. R. Donnelley & Sons.

Library of Congress Cataloging-in-Publication Data

Edelman, Gerald M.
  Wider than the sky : the phenomenal gift of
consciousness / Gerald M. Edelman.
      p.   cm.
Includes bibliographical references and index.
  ISBN 0-300-10229-1 (alk. paper)
  1. Consciousness—Physiological aspects. 2.
Brain—Physiology. I. Title.
QP411 .E346 2004
153—dc22   2003021089

A catalogue record for this book is available from the
British Library.

The paper in this book meets the guidelines for per-
manence and durability of the Committee on Production Guidelines for Book Longevity of the Council
on Library Resources.

10   9   8   7   6   5   4   3

For Maxine

The Brain—is wider than the Sky—
For—put them side by side—
The one the other will contain
With ease—and you—beside—

The Brain is deeper than the sea—
For—hold them—Blue to Blue—
The one the other will absorb—
As sponges—Buckets—do—

The Brain is just the weight of God—
For—Heft them—Pound for Pound—
And they will differ—if they do—
As Syllable from Sound—

Emily Dickinson, c. 1862

Contents

Preface   *xi*

Acknowledgments   *xv*

1. The Mind of Man: *Completing Darwin's Program*   1

2. Consciousness: *The Remembered Present*   4

3. Elements of the Brain   14

4. Neural Darwinism: *A Global Brain Theory*   32

5. The Mechanisms of Consciousness   48

6. Wider Than the Sky: *Qualia, Unity, and Complexity*   60

7. Consciousness and Causation: *The Phenomenal Transform*   76

8. The Conscious and the Nonconscious: *Automaticity and Attention*   87

9. Higher-Order Consciousness and Representation   97

10. Theory and the Properties of Consciousness   113

11. Identity: *The Self, Mortality, and Value*   131

12. Mind and Body: *Some Consequences*   140

    Glossary   149

    Bibliographic Note   181

    Index   187

Preface

Consciousness is the guarantor of all we hold to be human and precious. Its permanent loss is considered equivalent to death, even if the body persists in its vital signs. No wonder, then, that consciousness has attracted speculation and study across the ages. Over the past twenty-five years, I have written a number of books and papers on the subject. My conviction that consciousness is susceptible to scientific study has been supported by a sharp increase in the number of publications and scientific meetings on the subject.

These developments have prompted me to present an account of consciousness to the general reader. In carrying out this project, my goals were clear: to define consciousness and to offer as simple a view of the subject as is consistent with clarity. The subject is a challenging one and it will certainly require a concentrated effort on the part of the reader. I can only promise that the reward for such effort will be a deeper insight into issues that are at the center of human concern. Accordingly, except when absolutely necessary, I have deliberately omitted many scholarly references, which may be found in abundance in my previous works. Those interested in further reading can find a number of excellent works that have informed this book listed in the Bibliographic Note. I am aware that a great barrier to understanding scientific presentations rests in the inevitable use of technical terms. The problem is compounded when one considers details related to the brain and consciousness. For this reason, I have added a glossary that I hope will provide some alleviation.

William James, whose descriptions of consciousness still stand as a high-water mark in the field, said:

> Something definite happens when to a certain brain-state a certain "sciousness" corresponds. A genuine glimpse into what it is would be *the* scientific achievement, before which all past achievements would pale. But at the present, psychology is in the condition of physics before Galileo and the laws of motion, of chemistry before Lavoisier and the notion that mass is preserved in all reactions. The Galileo and the Lavoisier of psychology will be famous men indeed when they come, as come they some day surely will, or past successes are no index to the future. When they do come, however, the necessities of the case will make them "metaphysical." Meanwhile the best way in which we can facilitate their advent is to understand how great is the darkness in which we grope, and never forget that the natural-science

assumptions with which we started are provisional and revisable things.

I have puzzled over what James had in mind in stating that successful scientific efforts to glimpse the bases of consciousness would *necessarily* be metaphysical. In any event, in this book I have tried to avoid extensive discussion of metaphysical matters. I intend to deal with explanations that rest solely on a scientific base. My hope is to disenthrall those who believe the subject is exclusively metaphysical or necessarily mysterious.

A scientific analysis of consciousness must answer the question: How can the firing of neurons give rise to subjective sensations, thoughts, and emotions? To some, the two domains are so disparate as to be irreconcilable. A scientific explanation must provide a causal account of the connection between these domains so that properties in one domain may be understood in terms of events in the other. This is the task I have set myself in this small book.

The title of the book comes from a poem by Emily Dickinson that appears as the epigraph. This poem was written in around 1862, before modern brain science began toward the end of the nineteenth century. I find it impressive that, in extolling the width and depth of the mind, Dickinson referred exclusively to the brain. As for my subtitle, it is a play on the remarkable nature of consciousness, as well as on its rendering to us of the signals of this world.

Acknowledgments

I thank Drs. Kathryn Crossin, David Edelman, Joseph Gally, Ralph Greenspan, and George Reeke for their valuable criticism and useful suggestions. The illustrations were composed by Eric Edelman; I am grateful for his skilled and patient responses to my sometimes idiosyncratic suggestions. Darcie Plunkett provided excellent help in preparing this manuscript.

Chapter 1

The Mind of Man

COMPLETING DARWIN'S PROGRAM

*I*n 1869, Charles Darwin found himself vexed with his friend Alfred Wallace, the co-founder of the theory of evolution. They had differed on several issues related to that theory. But the main reason for Darwin's disturbance was a publication by Wallace concerning the origin of the brain and mind of man. Wallace, who by that time had spiritualist leanings, concluded that natural selection could not account for the human mind and brain.

Darwin wrote to him before publication: "I hope you have not murdered too completely your own and my child," meaning, of course, natural selection. Wallace, in fact, concluded that natural selection could not explain the origin of our higher intellectual and moral faculties. He claimed that savages and prehistoric humans had brains almost as large as those of Englishmen but, in adapting to an environment that did not require abstract thought, they had no use for such structures and therefore their brains could not have resulted from natural selection. Unlike Wallace, Darwin understood that such an adaptationist view, resting only on natural selection, was not cogent. He understood that properties and attributes not necessarily needed at one time could nevertheless be incorporated during the selection of other evolutionary traits. Moreover, he did not believe that mental faculties were independent of one another. As he explained in his book *The Descent of Man,* for example, the development of language might have contributed to the process of brain development.

This rich work has prevailed, along with Darwin's other views, but the program he established remains to be completed. One of the key tasks in completing that program is to develop a view of consciousness as a product of evolution rather than as a Cartesian substance, or *res cogitans,* a substance not accessible to scientific analysis. A major goal of this book is to develop such a view.

What is required to carry out such a project? Before answering this question, let us consider Darwin's entry in his notebook of 1838: "Origin of man now proved—metaphysic must flourish—He who understands baboon will do more towards metaphysics than Locke." These statements point in the direction we must follow. We must have a biological theory of consciousness and provide supporting evidence for that theory. The theory must show how the neural bases for consciousness could have arisen during evolution and how consciousness develops in certain animals.

Two subtle but important issues strongly influence our interpretation of these requirements. The first of these is the question of the causal status of consciousness. Some take the view that consciousness is a mere epiphenomenon with no material consequences. A contrary view is that consciousness is efficacious—that it causes things to happen. We will take the position, which we shall explore in detail later, that it suffices to show that the neural bases of consciousness, not consciousness itself, can cause things to happen. The second major challenge to any scientific account of consciousness is to show how a neural mechanism entails a subjective conscious state, or quale, as it is called. Before we can meet these two challenges, it is necessary to provide a sketch of the properties of consciousness and consider some matters of brain structure and function.

Chapter 2

Consciousness

THE REMEMBERED PRESENT

We all know what consciousness is: it is what you lose when you fall into a deep dreamless sleep and what you regain when you wake up. But this glib statement does not leave us in a comfortable position to examine consciousness scientifically. For that we need to explore the salient properties of consciousness in more detail, as William James did in his *Principles of Psychology*. Before doing so, it will help to clarify the subject if we first point out that consciousness is utterly dependent on the brain. The Greeks and others believed that consciousness resided in the heart, an idea that survives in many of our common metaphors. There is now a vast amount of empirical evidence to support the idea that consciousness emerges from the organization and operation of the brain. When brain function is curtailed—in deep anesthesia, after certain forms of brain trauma, after strokes, and in certain limited phases of sleep—consciousness is not present. There is no return of the functions of the body and brain after death, and post-mortem experience is simply not possible. Even during life there is no scientific evidence for a free-floating spirit or consciousness outside the body: consciousness is embodied. The question then becomes: What features of the body and brain are necessary and sufficient for consciousness to appear? We can best answer that question by specifying how the properties of conscious experience can emerge from properties of the brain.

Before taking up the properties of consciousness in this chapter, we must address another consequence of embodiment. This concerns the private or personal nature of each person's conscious experience. Here is James on the subject:

> In this room—this lecture room, say—there are a multitude of thoughts, yours and mine, some of which cohere mutually, and some not. They are as little each-for-itself and reciprocally independent as they are all-belonging-together. They are neither: no one of them is separate, but each

belongs with certain others and with none beside. My thought belongs with my other thoughts and your thought with your other thoughts. Whether anywhere in the room there be a mere thought, which is nobody's thought, we have no means of ascertaining, for we have no experience of the like. The only states of consciousness that we naturally deal with are found in (personal consciousness, minds, selves, concrete particular I's and you's.)

There is no mystery here. Since consciousness arrives as a result of each individual's brain and bodily functions, there can be no direct or collective sharing of that individual's unique and historical conscious experience. But this does not mean that it is impossible to isolate the salient features of that experience by observation, experiment, and report.

What is the most important statement one can make about consciousness from this point of view? It is that consciousness is a process, not a thing. James made this point trenchantly in his essay "Does Consciousness Exist?" To this day, many category errors have been made as a result of ignoring this point. For example, there are accounts that attribute consciousness specifically to nerve cells (or "consciousness neurons") or to particular layers of the cortical mantle of the brain. The evidence, as we shall see, reveals that the process of consciousness is a dynamic accomplishment of the distributed activities of populations of neurons in many different areas of the brain. That an area may be essential or necessary for consciousness does not mean it is sufficient. Furthermore, a given neuron may contribute to conscious activity at one moment and not at the next.

There are a number of other important aspects of consciousness as a process that may be called Jamesian properties. James pointed out that consciousness occurs only in the individual (that is, it is private or subjective), that it appears to be continuous, albeit continually changing, that it has intentionality (a term referring to the fact that, generally, it is about things), and that it does not exhaust all aspects of the things or events to which it refers. This last property has a connection to the important matter of attention. Attention, particularly focal attention, modulates conscious states and directs them to some extent, but it is not the same as consciousness. I will return to this issue in later chapters.

One outstanding property is that consciousness is unitary or integrated, at least in healthy individuals. When I consider my conscious state at the time of this writing, it appears to be all of a piece. While I am paying attention to the act of writing, I am aware of a ray of sunlight, of a humming sound across the street, of a small discomfort in my legs at the edge of the chair, and even of a "fringe," as James called it, that is of objects and events barely sensed. It is usually not entirely possible to reduce this integrated scene to just one thing, say my pencil. Yet this unitary scene will change and differentiate according to outside stimuli or inner thoughts to yet another scene. The number of such differentiated scenes seems endless, yet each is unitary. The scene is not just wider than the sky, it can contain many disparate elements—sensations, perceptions, images, memories, thoughts, emotions, aches, pains, vague feelings, and so on. Looked at from the inside, consciousness seems continually to change, yet at each moment it is all of piece—what I have called "the remembered present"—reflecting the fact that all my past experience is engaged in forming my integrated awareness of this single moment.

This integrated yet differentiated state looks entirely different to an outside observer, who possesses his or her own such states. If an outside observer tests whether I can consciously carry out more than two tasks simultaneously, he will find that my performance deteriorates. This apparent limitation of conscious capability, which is in contrast to the vast range of different inner conscious states, deserves analysis. I will consider its origins when I discuss the difference between conscious and nonconscious activity.

So far, I have not mentioned a property that is certainly obvious to all humans who are conscious. We are conscious of being conscious. (Indeed, it is just such a form of consciousness that impels the writing of this book.) We have scant evidence that other animals possess this ability; only higher primates show signs of it. In the face of this fact, I believe that we need to make a distinction between primary consciousness and higher-order consciousness. Primary consciousness is the state of being mentally aware of things in the world, of having mental images in the present. It is possessed not only by humans but also by animals lacking semantic or linguistic capabilities whose brain organization is nevertheless similar to ours. Primary consciousness is not accompanied by any sense of a socially defined self with a concept of a past or a future. It exists primarily in the remembered present. In contrast, higher-order consciousness involves the ability to be conscious of being conscious, and it allows the recognition by a thinking subject of his or her own acts and affections. It is accompanied by the ability in the waking state explicitly to re-create past episodes and to form future intentions. At a minimal level, it requires semantic ability, that is, the assignment of meaning to a symbol. In its most developed form, it requires linguistic ability, that is, the mastery of a whole system of symbols and a grammar. Higher primates, to some minimal degree, are assumed to have it, and in its most developed form it is distinctive of humans. Both cases require an internal ability to deal with tokens or symbols. In any event, an animal with higher-order consciousness necessarily must also possess primary consciousness.

There are different levels of consciousness. In rapid eye movement (REM) sleep, for example, dreams are conscious states. In contrast with individuals in the waking state, however, the dreaming individual is often gullible, is generally not conscious of being conscious, is not connected to sensory input, and is not capable of motor output. In deep or slow-wave sleep, short dreamlike episodes may occur, but for long periods there is no evidence of consciousness. In awaking from the unconsciousness induced by trauma or anesthesia, there may be confusion and disorientation. And, of course, there may be diseases of consciousness, such as schizophrenia, in which hallucinations, delusions, and disorientation can occur.

In the normal conscious state, individuals experience qualia. The term "quale" refers to the particular experience of some property—of greenness, for instance, or warmth, or painfulness. Much has been made of the need for providing a theoretical description that will allow us directly to comprehend qualia as experiences. But given that only a being with an individual body and brain can experience qualia, this kind of description is not possible. Qualia are high-order discriminations that constitute consciousness. It is essential to understand that differences in qualia are based on differences in the wiring and activity of parts of the nervous system. It is also valuable to understand that qualia are always experienced as parts of the unitary and integrated conscious scene. Indeed, all conscious events involve a complex of qualia. In general, it is not possible to experience only a single quale—"red," say—in isolation.

I shall elaborate later on the statement that qualia reflect the ability of conscious individuals to make high-order discriminations. How does such an ability reflect the efficacy of the neural states accompanying conscious experience? Imagine an animal with primary consciousness in the jungle. It hears a low growling noise, and at the same time the wind shifts and the light begins to wane. It quickly runs away, to a safer location. A physicist might not be able to detect any necessary causal relation among these events. But to an animal with primary consciousness, just such a set of simultaneous events might have accompanied a previous experience, which included the appearance of a tiger. Consciousness allowed integration of the present scene with the animal's past history of conscious experience, and that integration has survival value whether a tiger is present or not. An animal without primary consciousness might have many of the individual responses that the conscious animal has and might even survive. But, on average, it is more likely to have lower chances of survival—in the same environment it is less able than the conscious animal to discriminate and plan in light of previous and present events.

In succeeding chapters, I will attempt to explain how conscious scenes and qualia arise as a result of brain dynamics and experience. At the outset, though, it is important to understand what a scientific explanation of conscious properties can and cannot do. The issue concerns the so-called explanatory gap that arises from the remarkable differences between brain structure in the material world and the properties of qualia-laden experience. How can the firing of neurons, however complex, give rise to feelings, qualities, thoughts, and emotions? Some observers consider the two realms so widely divergent as to be impossible to reconcile. The key task of a scientific description of consciousness is to give a causal account of the relationship between these domains so that properties in one domain may be understood in terms of events in the other.

What such an explanation cannot and need not do is offer an explanation that replicates or creates any particular quale or experiential state. Science does not do that—indeed, imagine that a gifted scientist, through an understanding of fluid dynamics and meteorology, came up with a powerful theory of a complex world event like a hurricane. Implemented by a sophisticated computer model, this theory makes it possible to understand how hurricanes arise. Furthermore, with the computer model, the scientist could even predict most of the occurrences and properties of individual hurricanes. Would a person from a temperate zone without hurricanes, on hearing and understanding this theory, then expect to experience a hurricane or even get wet? The theory allows one to understand how hurricanes arise or are entailed by certain conditions, but it cannot create the experience of hurricanes. In the same way, a brain-based theory of consciousness should give a causal explanation of its properties but, having done so, it should not be expected to generate qualia "by description."

To develop an adequate theory of consciousness,

one must comprehend enough of how the brain works to understand phenomena, such as perception and memory, that contribute to consciousness. And if these phenomena can be causally linked, one would hope to test their postulated connections to consciousness by experimental means. This means that one must find the neural correlates of consciousness. Before addressing these issues, let us turn first to the brain.

Chapter 3

Elements of the Brain

*T*he human brain is the most complicated material object in the known universe. I have already said that certain processes within the brain provide the necessary mechanisms underlying consciousness. In the past decade or so, many of these processes have been identified. Brain scientists have described an extraordinary layering of brain structures at levels ranging from molecules to neurons (the message-carrying cells of the brain), to entire regions, all affecting behavior. In describing those features of the brain necessary to our exploration I will not go into great detail. To provide a foundation for a biological theory of consciousness, however, we do need to consider certain basic information on brain structure and dynamics. This excursion will require some patience on the reader's part. It will be rewarded when we develop a picture of how the brain works.

This short survey on the brain will cover, in order, a global description of brain regions, some notion of their connectivity, the basics of the activity of neurons and their connections—the synapses—and a bit of the chemistry underlying neuronal activity. All this will be necessary to confront a number of critical questions and principles: Is the brain a computer? How is it built during development? How complex are its transactions? Are there new principles of organization unique to the brain that were selected during evolution? What parts of the brain are necessary and sufficient for consciousness to emerge? In addressing these questions, I shall use the human brain as my central reference. There are, of course, many similarities between our brains and those of other animal species, and when necessary I shall describe these similarities as well as any significant differences.

The human brain weighs about three pounds. Its most prominent feature is the overlying wrinkled and convoluted structure known as the cerebral cortex, which is plainly visible in pictures of the brain (Figure 1). If the cerebral cortex were unfolded (making the gyri, its protrusions, and the sulci, its clefts, disappear) it would have the size and thickness of a large table napkin. It would contain at least 30 billion neurons, or nerve

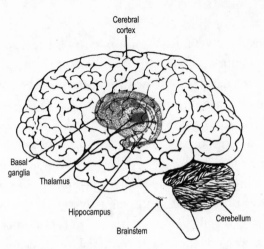

Figure 1. Relative locations of major parts of the human brain. The cerebral cortical mantle receives projections from the thalamus and sends reciprocal projections back; this constitutes the thalamocortical system. Beneath the mantle are three major cortical appendages—the basal ganglia, the hippocampus, and the cerebellum. Below them is the brainstem, evolutionarily the oldest part of the brain, which contains several diffusely projecting value systems.

cells, and 1 million billion connections, or synapses. If you started counting these synapses right now at a rate of one per second, you would just finish counting them 32 million years from now.

Neurons are connected to each other locally to form a dense network in portions of the brain called gray matter; they communicate over longer distances via fiber tracts called white matter. The cortex itself is a six-layered structure with different connection patterns in each layer. The cortex is subdivided into regions that mediate different sensory modalities, such as hearing, touch, and sight. There are other cortical regions dedicated to motor functions, the activity of which ultimately drives our muscles. Beyond the sensorimotor portions concerned with input and output, there are regions such as the frontal, parietal, and temporal cortices that are connected only to other parts of the brain and not to the outside world.

Before taking up other portions of the brain, I shall briefly describe in simplified form the structure and function of neurons and synapses. Different neurons can have a number of shapes, and there may be as many as two hundred or more different kinds in the brain. A neuron consists of a cell body with a diameter on the order of thirty microns, or about one ten-thousandth of an inch across (Figure 2). Neurons tend to be polar, with a treelike set of extensions called dendrites, and a long specialized extension called an axon, which connects the neuron to other neurons at synapses. The synapse is a specialized region that links the so-called presynaptic neuron (the neuron that sends a signal across the synapse) to a postsynaptic neuron (the neuron that receives the signal). The presynaptic portion of the synapse contains a special set of minute vesicles within which are chemicals known as neurotransmitters. Neurons possess an electrical charge as a result of their membrane properties, and when a neuron is excited current

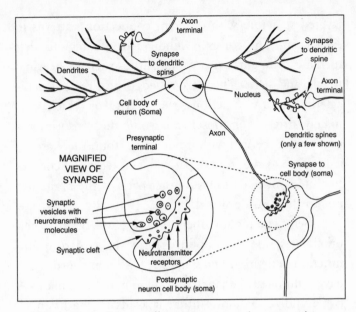

Figure 2. A diagram illustrating synaptic connections
between two neurons. An action potential traveling down
the axon of the presynaptic neuron causes the release of a
neurotransmitter into the synaptic cleft. The transmitter
molecules bind to receptors in the postsynaptic membrane,
changing the probability that the postsynaptic neuron
will fire. (Because of the number of different shapes
and kinds of neurons, this drawing is of necessity
a greatly simplified cartoon.)

flows through channels that open across the membrane.
As a result, a wave of electrical potential known as an
action potential moves from the cell body down the presynaptic axon and causes the release of neurotransmitter
molecules from vesicles into the synaptic cleft. These

molecules bind to molecular receptors or channels in the postsynaptic cell that, acting cumulatively, can cause it to fire an action potential of its own. Thus, neuronal communication occurs by a combination of controlled electrical and chemical events.

Now try to imagine the enormous numbers of neurons firing in various areas of the brain. Some firings are coherent (that is, they are simultaneous), others are not. Different brain regions have different neurotransmitters and chemicals whose properties change the timing, amplitude, and sequences of neuronal firing. To achieve and maintain the complex patterns of dynamic activity in healthy brains, some neurons are inhibitory, suppressing the firing of others, which are excitatory. Most excitatory neurons use the substance glutamate as their neurotransmitter, while the inhibitory neurons use GABA (gamma-aminobutyric acid). We can ignore the chemical details for now and simply accept that the effects of different chemical structures are different and that their distribution and occurrence together can have significant effects on neural activity.

I started by describing the cortex. With the picture of a polar neuron in mind, we can turn briefly to other key regions of the brain. One of the most important anatomical structures for understanding the origin of consciousness is the thalamus. This structure, which is located at the center of the brain, is essential for conscious function, even though it is only somewhat larger than the last bone in your own thumb. When nerves from different sensory receptors serving different modalities (located in your eyes, ears, skin, and so on) travel to your brain, they each connect in the thalamus with specific clusters of neurons called nuclei. Postsynaptic neurons in each specific thalamic nucleus then project axons that travel and map to particular areas of the cortex. A well-studied example is the projection from the neurons of the retina through the optic nerve to the part of the thalamus called the lateral geniculate nucleus and then to the primary visual cortical area, called V1 (for "visual area 1").

There is one striking feature of the many connections between the thalamus and the cortex: not only does the cortex receive many axons from thalamic neurons but there are also reciprocal axonal fibers going from the cortex back to the thalamus. We speak therefore of thalamocortical projections and corticothalamic projections. Reciprocal connections of this type abound within the cortex itself; such reciprocal connections are called corticocortical tracts. A striking example of these is the fiber bundle called the corpus callosum, which connects the two cortical hemispheres and consists of more than 200 million reciprocal axons. Cutting the corpus callosum leads to a split-brain syndrome, which in some cases can lead to the remarkable appearance of two separate and very different consciousnesses.

Each specific thalamic nucleus (and there are many) does not connect directly to any of the others. Surrounding the periphery of the thalamus, however, there is a layered structure called the reticular nucleus, which connects to the specific nuclei and which can inhibit their activity. The reticular nucleus, it is suspected, acts to switch or "gate" the activities of the specific thalamic nuclei, yielding different patterns of expression of such sensory modalities as sight, hearing, and touch. Another set of thalamic nuclei called intralaminar nuclei receive connections from certain lower structures in the brainstem that are concerned with activation of multiple neurons; these then project to many different areas of the cortex. The activity of these intralaminar nuclei is suspected to be essential for consciousness in that it sets appropriate thresholds or levels of cortical response—with too high a threshold, consciousness would be lost.

We may now turn to some other brain structures that are important to our efforts to track down the neural bases of consciousness. These are large subcortical regions that include the hippocampus, the basal ganglia, and the cerebellum. The hippocampus is an evolutionarily ancient cortical structure lined up like a pair of curled sausages along the inner skirt of the temporal cortex, one on the right side and another on the left. In cross section, each sausage looks like a sea horse, hence the name "hippocampus." Studies of the neural properties of the hippocampus provide important examples of some of the synaptic mechanisms underlying memory. One such mechanism, which should *not* be equated with memory itself, is the change in the strength, or efficacy, of hippocampal synapses that occurs with certain patterns of neural stimulation. As a result of this change, which can be either positive for long-term potentiation or negative for long-term depression, certain neural pathways are dynamically favored over others.

The point to be stressed is that, while synaptic change is essential for the function of memory, memory is a system property that also depends on specific neuro-anatomical connections.

Increased synaptic strength or efficacy within a pathway leads to a higher likelihood of conduction across that pathway, whereas decreases in synaptic strength diminish that likelihood. Various patterns have been found for the so-called synaptic rules governing these changes, following the initial proposals of Donald Hebb, a psychologist, and Friedrich von Hayek, an economist who, as a young man, thought quite a bit about how the brain works. These scholars suggested that an increase in synaptic efficacy would occur when pre- and postsynaptic neurons fired in close temporal order. Various modifications of this fundamental rule have been seen in different parts of the nervous system. What is particularly striking about the hippocampus, where these rules have been studied in detail, is the fact that bilateral removal of this structure leads to a loss of episodic memory, the memory of specific episodes or experiences in life. A very famous patient, H. M., whose hippocampi were removed to cure epileptic seizures, could not, for example, convert his short-term memory of events into a permanent narrative record, a condition that was depicted dramatically in the movie *Memento*. It is believed that such a long-term record results when particular synaptic connections between the hippocampus and the cortex are strengthened. When these connections are severed, the corresponding cortical synaptic changes cannot take place and the ability to remember episodes over the long term is lost. Such a patient can remember episodes up to the time of the operation, but loses long-term memory thereafter. It is intriguing that in some animals, such as rodents, hippocampal function is necessary for memories of a sense of place. In the absence of hippocampal functions, the animal cannot remember target places that have been explored.

All of the discussion so far has focused on sensory or cognitive functioning. The brain's motor functions, however, are also critically important, not just for the regulation of movement, but also for forming images and concepts, as we shall see. A key output area is the primary motor cortex, which sends signals down through the spinal cord to the muscles. There are also many other motor areas in the cortex, and there are nuclei in the thalamus related to motor function as well. Another structure related to motor functions is the cerebellum, a prominent bulb at the base of the cortex and above the brainstem (see Figure 1). The cerebellum appears to serve in the coordination and sequencing of motor actions and sensorimotor loops. There is no evidence, however, that it participates directly in conscious activity.

An intriguing set of structures known as the basal ganglia is critically important for motor control and sequencing. Lesions of certain structures in these nuclei lead to a loss of the neurotransmitter dopamine, and thus to the symptoms of Parkinson's syndrome. Patients with this disease have tremors, difficulty in initiating motor activity, rigidity, and even certain mental symptoms. The basal ganglia, as shown in Figure 1, are located in the center of the brain and connect to the cortex via the thalamus. Their neural connectivity, which is radically different from that of the cortex, consists of circuits of successive synapses or polysynaptic loops connecting the various ganglia. For the most part, the reciprocal connection patterns seen in the cortex itself and between the cortex and the thalamus are lacking in the basal ganglia. Moreover, most of the activity of the basal ganglia is through inhibitory neurons using GABA as a neurotransmitter. Nevertheless, since inhibition of inhibition (or disinhibition) can occur in these loops, they can stimulate target neurons as well as suppress their activity.

The basal ganglia are believed to be involved in the initiation and control of motor patterns. It is also likely that much of what is called procedural memory (remembering how to ride a bicycle, for example) and other nonconscious learned activity depends on the functions of the basal ganglia. As we shall see later, the regulatory functions of basal ganglia are also significant for forming categories of perceptions during experience.

There is one final set of structures that is critical in brain activity connected with learning and the maintenance of consciousness. These are the ascending systems, which my colleagues and I have called value systems because their activity is related to rewards and responses necessary for survival. They each have a different neurotransmitter, and from their nuclei of origin they send axons up and down the nervous system in a diffuse spreading pattern. These nuclei include the locus coeruleus, a relatively small number of neurons in the brainstem that release noradrenaline; the raphé nucleus, which releases serotonin; the various cholinergic nuclei, so-called because they release acetylcholine; the dopaminergic nuclei, which release dopamine; and the histaminergic system, which resides in a subcortical region called the hypothalamus, a region that affects many critical body functions.

The striking feature of such value systems is that, by projecting diffusely, each affects large populations of neurons simultaneously by releasing its neurotransmitter in the fashion of a leaky garden hose. By doing so, these systems affect the probability that neurons in the neighborhood of value-system axons will fire after receiving glutamatergic input. These systems bias neuronal responses affecting both learning and memory and controlling bodily responses necessary for survival. It is for this reason that they are termed value systems. In addition, there are other loci in the brain with modulatory functions mediated by substances called neuropeptides. An example is enkephalin, an endogenous opioid that regulates responses to pain. In addition, there are other brain areas, such as the amygdala, which are involved in emotional responses, such as fear. For our purposes, these areas need not be described in detail.

To summarize our account so far, we may say that, in a gross sense, there are three main neuroanatomical motifs in our brains (Figure 3). The first is the thalamocortical motif, with tightly connected groups of neurons connected both locally and across distances by rich reciprocal connections. The second is the polysynaptic loop structure of the inhibitory circuits of the basal

---

Figure 3. Fundamental arrangements of three kinds of neuroanatomical systems in the brain. The top diagram shows the gross topology of the thalamocortical system, which is a dense meshwork of reentrant connectivity between the cortex and the thalamus and among different cortical areas. The middle diagram shows the long polysynaptic loops connecting the cortex with subcortical structures such as the basal ganglia. In this case, these loops go from the basal ganglia to the thalamus, thence to the cortex and back from the target areas of cortex to the ganglia. These loops are, in general, not reentrant. The bottom diagram shows one of the diffusely projecting value systems, in which the locus coeruleus distributes a "hairnet" of fibers all over the brain. These fibers release the neuromodulator noradrenaline when the locus coeruleus is activated.

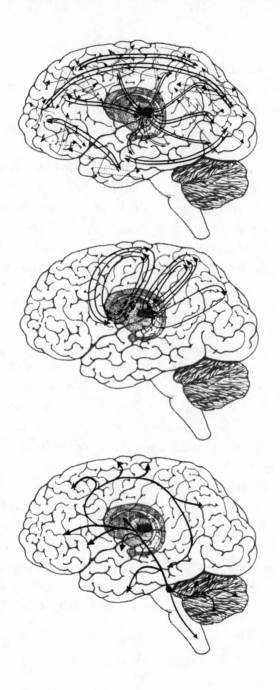

ganglia. The third consists of the diffuse ascending projections of the different value systems. Of course, this generalization is a gross oversimplification, given the exquisite detail and individuation of neural circuitry. But as we shall see, it provides a useful simplification; we can dispose of it once we have seen its uses.

So much for simplicity. The picture I have painted so far only hints at the remarkably complex dynamics of the neural structures of the brain. After staring at the gross layout of brain regions in Figure 1 and understanding the synapse pictured in Figure 2, close your eyes and imagine myriad neural firings in millions of pathways. Some of this neural activity would occur at certain frequencies while others would show variable frequencies. Bodily activity and signals from the environment and the brain itself would modify which of the pathways were favored over others as a result of changes in synaptic strength. Although I hardly expect the reader to be able to visualize precisely the hyperastronomical numbers of neural patterns in detail, perhaps this exercise will yield a further appreciation of the brain's complexity.

We are now in a position to address some of the questions posed at the beginning of this chapter. Consider the question of whether the brain is a computer. If we examine how neural circuits are built during animal development, this would seem unlikely. The brain arises during development from a region of the embryo called the neural tube. Progenitor cells (cells that are precursors to neurons and support cells called glia) move in certain patterns to make various layers and patterns. As they differentiate into neurons, many also die. From the very beginning of neuroanatomy, there are rich statistical variations in both cell movement and cell death. As a result, no two individuals, not even identical twins, possess the same anatomical patterns.

In the earliest stages of development, the cellular organization characteristic of a species is controlled by families of genes among which are the so-called *Hox* genes and *Pax* genes. But at a certain point, the control of neural connectivity and fate becomes epigenetic; that is, it is not prespecified as "hardwiring," but rather is guided by patterns of neural activity. Neurons that fire together wire together. While, at earlier stages, patterned cell movement and programmed cell death determine anatomical structure, the movement and death of individual neurons are nonetheless statistically variable or stochastic. The same holds for which particular neurons connect to each other at later stages. The result is a pattern of constancy and variation leading to highly individual networks in each animal. This is no way to build a computer, which must execute input algorithms or effective procedures according to a precise prearranged program and with no error in wiring.

There are other, even more trenchant reasons for rejecting the idea of digital computation as a basis for brain action. As we shall see later, what would be lethal noise for a computer is in fact critical for the operation of higher-order brain functions. For the moment, though, let us consider some other aspects of brain complexity and its relation to brain structure and function.

A review of what I have said about the overall arrangement of brain areas might tempt one to conclude that the key to brain function is modularity. Since there are regions that are functionally segregated for vision (even for color, movement, and orientation), for example, or similarly for hearing or touch, we might be tempted to conclude that specific brain action is mainly the result of the specialized functioning of these isolated local parts or modules. If pushed to higher levels, this simple notion results in phrenology, the picture of localized separate brain faculties first proposed by Franz Joseph Gall. We now know that modularity of this kind is indefensible. The alternative picture, that the brain operates only as a whole (the holistic view), will also not stand up to scrutiny.

The notion of modularity is based on an overly simple interpretation of the effects of ablation of parts of the brain, either by animal experiments or as a result of a stroke, or of surgery for epilepsy. It is clear, for example, that ablation of cortical area V1 leads to blindness. It does not follow, however, that all the properties of vision are assured by the functioning of V1, which is the first cortical area in a series making up the visual pathway. Similarly, although modern imaging techniques reveal certain areas of the brain that are active in certain tasks, it does not follow that the activity of such areas is the *sole* cause of particular behaviors. Necessity is not sufficiency. But the contrary or holistic argument is not tenable either—one must account for both integration *and* differentiation of brain activity. This will be one of our main tasks in proposing a global brain theory. As we shall see later, the long-standing argument between localizationists and holists dissolves if one considers how the functionally segregated regions of the brain are connected as a complex system in an intricate but integrated fashion. This integration is essential to the emergence of consciousness.

This reasoning is critical to understanding the relationship between brain function and consciousness. Of course, there are areas of the brain that if damaged or removed will lead to permanent unconsciousness. One such area is the midbrain reticular formation. Another is the region of the thalamus containing the intralaminar nuclei. These structures are not the site of consciousness, however. As a process, consciousness needs their activity, but to account for the Jamesian properties of consciousness requires a much more dynamic picture involving integration of the activities of multiple brain regions. We are now in a position to lay the groundwork for just such a picture by considering a global brain theory that accounts for the evolution, development, and function of this most complex of organs.

Chapter 4

Neural Darwinism

A GLOBAL BRAIN THEORY

*T*here is one simple principle that governs how the brain works: it evolved; that is, it was not designed. As stated, this principle sounds almost simple-minded, doesn't it? But we must not forget that, although evolution is not intelligent, it is enormously powerful. The power comes from natural selection acting in complex environments over eons of time. A key idea developed by Darwin is embedded in his notion of population thinking: functioning structures and whole organisms emerge as a result of selection among the diverse variant individuals in a population, which compete with one another for survival. I hold this notion to be central, not only in considering how the brain has evolved, but also in thinking about how it develops and functions. Applying population thinking to understanding how the brain works leads to a global theory, called neural Darwinism or the theory of neuronal group selection.

What do we mean by the term "global" and why do we need a global brain theory? An explanation of consciousness will necessarily require an understanding of perception, memory, action, and intention—in short, an *overall* understanding of how the brain works that goes beyond the functioning of one brain region or another. Given the richness, variety, and range of conscious experience, it is also important to construct a brain theory that is principled and compatible with evolution and development. By principled, I mean a theory that describes the principles governing the major mechanisms by which the brain deals with information and novelty. One such theory or model is the idea that the brain is like a computer or Turing machine. In contrast to such an instructive model, which relies on programs and algorithms, models based on population thinking rely on selection of particular elements or states from a large repertoire of variant elements or states. Explanations of consciousness based on one or the other of these two kinds of models differ greatly. By now, it should be no mystery that I prefer selectional models based on population thinking.

The reason population thinking is important in determining how the brain works has to do with the extraordinary amount of variation in each individual brain. This is true at all levels of structure and function. Different individuals have different genetic influences, different epigenetic sequences, different bodily responses, and different histories in varying environments. The result is enormous variation at the levels of neuronal chemistry, network structure, synaptic strengths, temporal properties, memories, and motivational patterns governed by value systems. In the end, there are obvious differences from person to person in the contents and styles of their streams of consciousness. The variability of individual nervous systems was commented on by the distinguished neuroscientist Karl Lashley, who admitted that he had no ready explanation for the existence of so much variation. Even though there are general patterns exhibited by the brain in the face of this variation, it cannot be dismissed as mere noise. There is too much of it, and it exists at too many levels of organization—molecules, cells, and circuits. It is simply not likely that evolution, like a computer programmer dealing with noise, could have devised multiple error-correcting codes to assure preservation of patterns in the brain by counteracting this enormous variation.

An alternative way of confronting neural variability is to consider it fundamental and to assume that the individual local differences within each brain make up populations of variants. In this case, selection from such a population of variants could lead to patterns even under unpredictable circumstances, provided that some constraint of value or fitness was satisfied. In evolution, fitter individuals survive and have more progeny. In the individual brain, those synaptic populations that match value systems or rewards are more likely to survive or contribute more to the production of future behavior.

This view is in sharp contrast to computer models of the brain and mind. According to these models, signals from the environment carry input information that is unambiguous, once contaminating noise is averaged away or otherwise dealt with. These models assume that the brain has a set of programs, or so-called effective procedures, which are capable of changing states based on the information carried by the inputs, yielding functionally appropriate outputs. Such models are instructive in the sense that information from the world is assumed to elicit the formation of appropriate responses based on logical deduction. These models do not deal, however, with the fact that inputs to the brain are not unambiguous—the world is not like a piece of tape with a fixed sequence of symbols for the brain to read. I have already mentioned the challenge to computer models of the brain posed by the richly variable circuitry of real brains.

There is also a set of functional issues that make computer models unlikely. For example, the mapped connections from the sense of touch in the hand through the thalamus to the region of somatosensory cortex are variable and plastic, even in adults. The subregions in the somatosensory cortex mapping the fingers dynamically shift all their boundaries as a result of excessive use of even one finger—a shift in the *context* of use. Similar phenomena reflecting such context dependence and dynamic circuit variation are seen for other senses. Furthermore, in sensory systems such as that for vision, there are multiple cortical regions that are each functionally segregated, for example, for color, movement, orientation, and so on. These functionally specialized areas can exceed thirty in number and are distributed all over the brain. Yet there is no superordinate area or executive program binding the color, edge, form, and movement of an object into a coherent percept. This binding is not explicable by invoking a visual computer program operating according to the principles of artificial intelligence. A coherent percept in fact nevertheless emerges in various contexts, and explaining how this occurs constitutes the so-called binding problem. A global brain theory must provide a cogent solution to this problem by proposing an appropriate mechanism. It will soon become clear that such a solution is central to our understanding of consciousness.

To emphasize the dependence of perception on context, we may call upon the huge phenomenology of illusions, visual and otherwise. One example is the Kanizsa pattern, which consists of the angular portions of a triangle, disconnected, but appears to show an overlying triangle with sharp boundaries (Figure 4). Yet there is no true energy difference in the light that is

Figure 4. Illusory contours in a Kanizsa triangle. Most people report the appearance of a distinct triangular shape and an increase in apparent luminance within the triangle, but neither of these features exists in the physical image.

received from the two sides of the contour that is perceived. Such a contour is called "illusory." The brain constructs the contour, which, by the way, is not necessarily a straight line but can be curved depending on the context of the particular figure used.

Many other functional responses of the perceiving animal could be described to illustrate why an a priori program is not a likely explanation for physiological or psychological properties. I shall mention only two more. The first is the remarkable tendency of brains to seek out closure and avoid gaps. In daily life, for example, you do not see the blind spot in your visual field occasioned by the presence of the optic nerve near the center of your retina. Even more striking phenomena come from the field of neuropsychology, which, among other things, studies responses to strokes. This field is replete with examples of closure phenomena that can even be delusional. A most exotic example is anosognosia, a syndrome in which a paralyzed patient does not recognize the existence of paralysis even if it involves his or her entire left side. In such cases, we see extraordinary adaptation and integration by the damaged brain as it responds to the loss of cortical areas.

In addition to construction and closure, and possibly in connection with them, the brain's capacity to generalize is astonishing. A case in point is the ability of pigeons, when appropriately rewarded, to look at numerous photographs of various fish species in different scales and contexts and learn to positively recognize the similarity in the photographs. Pigeons trained at this task can recognize that these diverse pictures have something in common more than 80 percent of the time. It is highly unlikely that this behavior is the result of a fixed template or a set of predetermined algorithms in the brains of pigeons. Nor can it be explained by natural selection for the positive recognition of fish. Pigeons neither evolve with fish nor live with them, and they don't eat them either.

I could cite many more examples ranging from the developmental anatomy of the brain to the individual variation of brain scans in humans carrying out similar tasks. But the conclusion is clear: the brains of higher-level animals autonomously construct patterned responses to environments that are full of novelty. They do not do this the way a computer does—using formal rules governed by explicit, unambiguous instructions or input signals. Once more, with feeling: the brain is not a computer, and the world is not a piece of tape.

If the brain is in fact not a computer and the world is not a piece of tape, how can the brain operate so as to yield adaptive and patterned responses? As I have already suggested, the answer lies in a selectionist theory that I have called the theory of neuronal group selection, or TNGS (Figure 5). This theory has three tenets: (1) Developmental selection—during the early establishment of neuroanatomy, epigenetic variations in the patterns of connections among growing neurons create repertoires in each brain area consisting of millions of variant circuits or neuronal groups. The variations arise at the level of synapses as a result of the fact that neurons that fire together wire together during the embryonic and fetal stages of development. (2) Experiential selection—overlapping this first phase of selection and after the major neuroanatomy is built, large variations in synaptic strengths, positive and negative, result from variations in environmental input during behavior. These synaptic modifications are subject to the constraints of value systems described in the previous chapter. (3) Reentry—during development, large numbers of reciprocal connections are established both locally and over long distances. This provides a basis for signaling between mapped areas across such reciprocal fibers. Reentry is

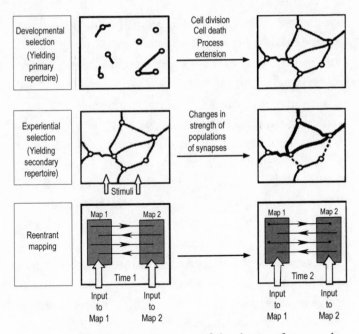

Figure 5. The three main tenets of the theory of neuronal group selection, or neural Darwinism: (1) Developmental selection leads to a highly diverse set of circuits, one of which is shown. (2) Experiential selection leads to changes in the connection strengths of synapses, favoring some pathways (thickened black lines) and weakening others (dashed lines). (3) Reentrant mapping, in which brain maps are coordinated in space and time through ongoing reentrant signaling across reciprocal connections. The black dots in the maps on the right indicate strengthened synapses. As a result of (1) and (2), a myriad of circuits and functioning pathways is created constituting a repertoire for selectional events. The further and ongoing events of reentry in (3) must be thought of as dynamic and recursive, mapping the maps over time.

the ongoing recursive interchange of parallel signals among brain areas, which serves to coordinate the activities of different brain areas in space and time. Unlike feedback, reentry is not a sequential transmission of an error signal in a simple loop. Instead, it simultaneously involves many parallel reciprocal paths and has no prescribed error function attached to it.

The consequence of this dynamic process is the widespread synchronization of the activity of widely distributed neuronal groups. It binds their functionally segregated activities into circuits capable of coherent output. In the absence of logic (the organizing principle of computers as instructive systems), reentry is the central organizing principle that governs the spatiotemporal coordination among multiple selectional networks of the brain. This solves the binding problem that I mentioned earlier. Through reentry, for example, the color, orientation, and movement of a visual object can be integrated. No superordinate map is necessary to coordinate and bind the activities of the various individual maps that are functionally segregated for each of these attributes. Instead, they coordinate by communicating directly with each other, through reentry.

The three tenets of the TNGS together form a selectional system. Prominent examples of selectional systems include evolution, the immune system, and complex nervous systems. All follow a set of three guiding principles. The first principle assumes a means for generating diversity in a population of elements, whether of individuals or of cells. The second is a means allowing extensive encounters between individuals in a variant population or repertoire and the system that is to be recognized, whether it is an ecological environment, a foreign molecule, or a set of sensory signals. The third principle is some means to differentially amplify the number, survival, or influence of those elements in the diverse repertoire that happen to meet selective criteria. In evolution, these are criteria of fitness allowing the differential survival and breeding of certain individuals—the process of natural selection itself. In immunity, amplification occurs through the enhanced division of just those clones of immune cells having antibodies on their surface that bind particular foreign molecules or antigens well enough to exceed a certain critical energy of binding. In neural systems, amplification consists of enhancing the strengths of those synapses and circuits of neuronal groups that meet the criteria set by value systems. It is the neuronal groups made up of excitatory and inhibitory neurons in particular anatomical patterns rather than individual neurons that are selected.

Notice that while these three different selectional systems obey similar *principles,* they use different *mechanisms* to achieve successful matching to various unforeseen inputs. Evolution is, of course, special and overarching because it is also responsible for actually selecting the different mechanisms used by the immune and nervous systems. It tends to favor those individuals that successfully utilize such mechanisms to improve their fitness and allow more of their progeny to survive.

Since the proposal of the TNGS in 1978, a growing body of evidence has supported the notion that neuronal groups connected by reentrant interactions are the selectional units in higher-level brains. This evidence is presented in a number of books and papers and will not be reviewed here. Instead, I will consider certain consequences of the theory that are particularly important for understanding the mechanisms underlying consciousness.

One important consequence is that the brain is so versatile in its responses because those responses are degenerate. Degeneracy is the ability of structurally different elements of a system to perform the same function or yield the same output. A clear-cut example is seen in the genetic code. The code is made up of triplets of nucleotide bases, of which there are four kinds: G, C, A, and T. Each triplet, or codon, specifies one of the twenty different amino acids that make up a protein. Since there are sixty-four different possible codons—actually sixty-one, if we leave out three stop codons—which makes a total of more than one per amino acid, the code words are degenerate. For example, the third position of many triplet codons can contain any one of the four letters or bases without changing their coding specificity. If it takes a sequence of three hundred codons to specify a sequence of one hundred amino acids in a protein, then a large number of different base sequences in messages (approximately 3^{100}) can specify the same amino-acid sequence. Despite their different structures at the level of nucleotides, these degenerate messages yield the same protein.

Degeneracy is a ubiquitous biological property. It requires a certain degree of complexity, not only at the genetic level as I have illustrated above, but also at cellular, organismal, and population levels. Indeed, degeneracy is necessary for natural selection to operate and it is a central feature of immune responses. Even identical twins who have similar immune responses to a foreign agent, for example, do not generally use identical combinations of antibodies to react to that agent. This is because there are many structurally different antibodies with similar specificities that can be selected in the immune response to a given foreign molecule.

Degeneracy is particularly important in helping to solve major problems in complex nervous systems. I have already mentioned the binding problem. How can it be that, despite the absence of a computer program, executive function, or superordinate map, up to thirty-three functionally segregated and widely distributed visual maps in the brain can nevertheless yield perception that coherently binds edges, orientations, colors, and movement into one perceptual image? How do different maps for color, orientation, object movement, and so on correlate or coordinate their responses? As I suggested above, the answer lies in mutual reentrant interactions that, for a time, link various neuronal groups in each map to those of others to form a functioning circuit. Simulations show that the neurons that yield such circuits fire more or less in phase with each other, or synchronously. But in the next time period, different neurons and neuronal groups may form a structurally different circuit, which nevertheless has the same output. And again, in the succeeding time period, a new circuit is formed using some of the same neurons, as well as completely new ones in different groups. These different circuits are degenerate—they are different in structure but they yield similar outputs to solve the binding problem (Figure 6).

Within each particular circuit, the different neuronal groups fire synchronously. The different circuits yielding the same output are not, however, synchronous or in phase with each other, nor do they have to be. As a result of reentry, the properties of synchrony and coherency allow more than one structure to give a similar output. As long as such degenerate operations occur in succession to link distributed populations of neuronal groups, there is no need for an executive or superordinate program as there would be in a computer.

The formulation of a global brain theory like the TNGS, while essential to understanding how the brain works, does not solve all of the detailed mechanistic problems related to the local operations of networks in the various nuclei and regions of the brain. But it does remove the paradoxes that arise if one assumes that the brain functions like a computer. One such paradox

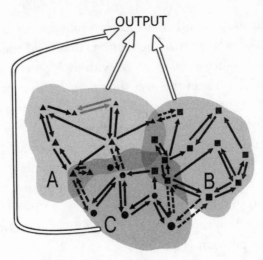

OUTPUT

Outputs: At time t,   C
At time t+1,   A
At time t+2,   B

Figure 6. Illustration of the degeneracy of reentrant circuits in the brain. Even though the three overlapping circuits in A, B, and C are different, as shown by the shading, they can yield a similar output over some period of time.

would have us imagine a cell with a designated categorical function that dominates the function of all subordinate neurons connected to it—for example, a cell that fires when you think of a particular person, a so-called grandmother cell. Such a cell is not necessary in this theory. Different cells can carry out the same function and the same cell can, at two different times, carry out different functions in different neuronal groups. Moreover, given the selectional nature of higher-order interactions in the brain, one does not have to invoke a homunculus, a little man who lives in the brain, to interpret the meaning of a percept. Just as Darwin's theory of natural selection disposed of the argument from design, the TNGS disposes of the need for either a fixed instructional plan or a homunculus in the head.

These issues are directly relevant to my next task, which is to show how the principles and mechanisms of the TNGS can be used to understand the origin of consciousness.

Chapter 5

The Mechanisms of Consciousness

My fundamental assumption has been that the process of consciousness arises from the workings of the brain. I must show how that can occur as an evolutionary event connecting previously evolved capabilities with new structural and functional features that emerge as a result of natural selection. To do so, I must dissect the necessary components whose interactions result in the appearance of primary consciousness—the ability to construct a scene in a discriminative fashion. Thus, before proposing mechanisms of consciousness, I will consider the contributory brain processes that are essential for these mechanisms to operate.

One of the most basic processes in higher brains is the ability to carry out perceptual categorization—to "make sense" of the world. This ability allows an animal to carve up the world of signals coming from the body and the environment into sequences that result in adaptive behavior. For example, we continually take in the parallel and multiple visual signals from a room and categorize them as coherent stable objects ("chairs," "tables," and so forth). A cat might do such a categorization but with different perceptual and motor responses (it might jump on the object we call a table). And a cockroach might treat that same object as a place to hide in the darkness of the table's underside.

In the mammalian nervous system, perceptual categorization is carried out by interactions between sensory and motor systems in what I have called global mappings. A global mapping is a dynamic structure containing various sensory maps, each with different functionally segregated properties, linked by reentry. These are linked in turn by non-reentrant connections to motor maps and subcortical systems such as the cerebellum and basal ganglia. The function of a global mapping is first to sample the world of signals by movement and attention and then to categorize these signals as coherent through reentry and synchronization of neuronal groups. Such a structure, consisting of both sensory and motor components, is the main basis for perceptual categorization in higher brains.

While perceptual categorization is fundamental, it cannot itself give rise to generalization across various signal complexes to yield the properties that the signals have in common. For such generalization, the brain must map its own activities, as represented by several global mappings, to create a concept—that is, to make maps of its perceptual maps. For example, to register forward motion, a cat's nervous system might map its own activities as "cerebellum and basal ganglia active in pattern a, premotor and motor regions active in pattern b, and submodalities in visual maps active in patterns x, y, and z." Note that although I have, for purposes of illustration, expressed this generalized mapping in the form of a proposition (or verbal expression), the operation in a cat's brain is obviously non-propositional. Higher-order cortical maps in the prefrontal, parietal, and temporal areas are likely to carry out this construction, which might correspond to a "universal," a *concept* of forward motion. No linear sum of global mappings could give rise to such a generalization. Instead, generalization arises by abstracting certain features of such mappings by means of higher-order maps.

Perceptual categorization and concept formation would not be adaptive to an animal in the absence of memory, and, as we shall see, the understanding of memory is essential for formulating a theory of consciousness. According to the TNGS, memory is the capacity to repeat or suppress a specific mental or physical act. It arises as a result of changes in synaptic efficacy (or synaptic strength) in circuits of neuronal groups. After such changes have occurred, they tend to favor the recruitment of certain of these circuits to yield re-enactment. This recruitment may occur in more than one way—that is, in a degenerate fashion. As we shall see, certain forms of memory require either relatively fast changes in synaptic efficacy or at least the ongoing activity of particular neural circuits in time periods of less than about one-third of a second. Other forms of memory require slower, but more stable, changes in synaptic strength.

Students of memory have categorized various memory systems in a useful fashion. They distinguish long-term memory from short-term, or working, memory by taking into account how long a particular memory lasts and the structures it depends on. Brain scientists also distinguish between procedural memory—that which reflects motor learning and its complex acts—from episodic memory, the ability to carry out long-term recall of sequences of events or narratives. As I have already mentioned, episodic memory depends on interactions between the hippocampus and the cerebral cortex. While these various classifications are very important and useful, it is likely that there are many additional systems of memory that remain to be described. Moreover, much remains to be done to uncover the interactions among the various memory systems.

There are a number of additional issues that we must clarify to understand how memory operates in higher brains. For example, memory cannot simply be equated with synaptic change, although changes in synaptic strength are essential for it. Instead, memory is a system property reflecting the effects of context and the associations of the various degenerate circuits capable of yielding a similar output. Thus, each event of memory is dynamic and context-sensitive—it yields a repetition of a mental or physical act that is similar but not identical to previous acts. It is recategorical: it does not replicate an original experience exactly. There is no reason to assume that such a memory is representational in the sense that it stores a static registered code for some act. Instead, it is more fruitfully looked on as a property of degenerate nonlinear interactions in a multidimensional network of neuronal groups. Such interactions allow a non-identical "reliving" of a set of prior acts and events, yet there is often the illusion that one is recalling an event exactly as it happened.

Two analogies are useful in clarifying this point. A representational memory would be like a coded inscription cut into a rock that is subsequently brought back into view and interpreted. A nonrepresentational memory would be like changes in a glacier influenced by changes in the weather, which are interpreted as signals. In the analogy, the melting and refreezing of the glacier represent changes in the synaptic response, the ensuing different rivulets descending the mountain terrain represent the neural pathways, and the pond into which they feed represents the output. Successive meltings and refreezings due to changes in the weather could lead to a degenerate set of paths of water descending in the rivulets, some of which might join and associate in novel ways. Occasionally, an entirely new pond might be created. In no case, however, is it likely that the same dynamic pattern will be repeated exactly, although the general consequences of changes in the pond below—the output state—could be quite similar. In this view, memories are necessarily associative and are never identical. Nevertheless, under various constraints they can be sufficiently effective in yielding the same output.

Recognizing that a dynamic memory system operates within the brain's selectional framework implies that it will be influenced by the changes in neural inputs that come from that brain's value systems. Indeed, notice that the mechanisms leading to perceptual categorization—global mappings, concept formation, and dynamic short-term memory—all call upon *interactions* of the three major motifs of global neural systems that were discussed in reviewing the neuroanatomy of higher brains in Chapter 3. These are the thalamocortical maps, the subcortical organs concerned with temporal succession (the hippocampus, basal ganglia, and cerebellum), and the diffuse ascending value systems. To reflect these interactions, I have called the central memory system a value-category memory system, one in which the constraints of value systems can determine the degree and extent of recall and output. Animals without consciousness still utilize all of the above systems, but they would lack the critical interactions leading to consciousness. In fact, it is a central tenet of the extended TNGS (the theory applied to consciousness) that the development of all these systems was a necessary evolutionary precursor of conscious activity.

We may now ask the critical question: what is the *sufficient* evolutionary event leading to the emergence of consciousness? The thesis I am proposing is that, at a point in evolutionary time corresponding to the transition between reptiles and birds and reptiles and mammals, a new reciprocal connectivity appeared in the thalamocortical system. Massively reentrant connectivity developed between the cortical areas carrying out perceptual categorization and the more frontal areas responsible for value-category memory based on fast changes in synaptic strength. Cortical reentry was mediated by the emergence of several grand systems of reentrant corticocortical connections linking distributed areas of the cortex. At the same time there was an increase in the reentrant connectivity with the thalamus, as well as an increase in the number of thalamic nuclei. The reentrant connections between the thalamus and cortex were enhanced, both for the specific thalamic nuclei and the intralaminar nuclei described in Chapter 3, while the reticular nucleus of the thalamus developed enhanced inhibitory circuits by which it connected to the specific nuclei. This allowed the activity of the reticular nucleus to gate or select various combinations of the activity of those specific thalamic nuclei corresponding to different sensory modalities. The intralaminar nuclei, which send diffuse connections to most areas of the cortex, helped to synchronize the new thalamocortical responses and regulate the overall levels of activity in these multiple reentrant systems (Figure 7).

These dynamic reentrant interactions in the thalamocortical system must be thought of as successive in time—new perceptual categorizations are reentrantly connected to memory systems before they themselves become part of an altered memory system. This bootstrapping between memory and perception is assumed to be stabilized within time periods ranging from hundreds of milliseconds to seconds—the so-called specious present of William James. I have called this period "the remembered present" to point up the dynamic interaction between memory and ongoing perception that gives rise to consciousness.

What is the consequence of this evolutionary development in which value-category memory was dynamically linked to perceptual categorization? It is the ability to construct a complex scene and to make discriminations between components of that scene. As an animal moves, engaging many global mappings in response to the world around it, the ongoing parallel signals reentrantly connecting different sensory modalities lead to correlations among complexes of perceptual cate-

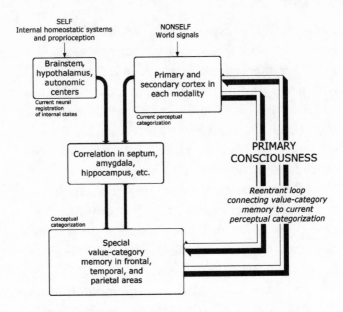

Figure 7. Reentrant pathways leading to primary
consciousness. Two main kinds of signals are critical—
those from "self," constituting value systems and regulatory
elements of the brain and body along with their sensory
components, and those from "nonself," signals from the
world that are transformed through global mappings. Signals
related to value and categorized signals from the outside
world are correlated and lead to memory, which is capable of
conceptual categorization. This "value-category" memory is
linked by reentrant paths (the heavy lines) to the current
perceptual categorization of world signals. This reentrant
linkage is the critical evolutionary development that results
in primary consciousness. When it occurs across many
modalities (sight, touch, and so forth), primary consciousness
is of a "scene" made up of responses to objects and events,
some of which are not necessarily causally connected to
each other. An animal with primary consciousness can
nonetheless discriminate and connect these objects and
events through the memory of its previous value-laden
experience. This ability enhances its survival value.

gories stimulated by objects and events. The ability to create a scene by such reentrant correlations between value-category memory—reflecting earlier categorizations—and similar or different perceptual categories is the basis for the emergence of primary consciousness.

Some of the earliest categorizations are related to signals from the animal's own body and brain. These signals come from autonomic and homeostatic systems that regulate vital organs and interactions of physiological functions such as breathing, eating, and hormonal changes. They are called autonomic because they do not depend on conscious control and are homeostatic because they compensate for changes in a balanced fashion. Other bodily signals come from muscles and joints and systems related to balance—so-called kinesthetic and proprioceptive systems. All of these systems continue to operate in the life of the animal, providing a central referential set of signals and perceptual categories to that individual. Signals from such "self" systems begin even before birth and remain as a central feature of primary consciousness. The salience of various elements contributing to the scene is governed by memories conditioned by the history of reward and punishment during the animal's past behavior. Such a history plays a key role in emotional responses and their associated feelings.

The ability to construct a conscious scene in a fraction of a second is the ability to construct a remembered present. Note that the causal or physical connection between several incoming signals is not necessarily a deciding issue in the animal's response to this construction. For example, as I have already mentioned, an animal in the jungle sensing a shift in sounds while the light is diminished in its immediate surroundings may flee, even if there is no causal correlation between these two inputs. It is sufficient that the combination of such simultaneous inputs in the past value-dependent history of that animal was previously accompanied by the presence, say, of a tiger. An animal without the gift of primary consciousness might survive for some time in such a niche but could not make the same discriminations on the basis of its rapidly changing value-category memory. Eventually, that animal is less likely to survive. By contrast, an animal with the ability to construct a scene can have a greater discriminatory capacity and selectivity in choosing its responses to novel and complex environments. The efficacy of its conscious systems and their possible contribution to increased fitness rests in their enormously increased discriminatory capacity.

The brief account given here refers to the emergence of mechanisms for primary consciousness. They are consistent with the observation that consciousness is an active process. As I shall discuss later, the subsequent evolution of additional reentrant circuits permitting the acquisition of semantic capability, and finally language, gave rise to higher-order consciousness in certain higher primates, including our hominine ancestors (and arguably a number of other ape species). Higher-order consciousness confers the ability to imagine the future, explicitly recall the past, and to be conscious of being conscious. While I shall not consider the details at this point, it is necessary to use the example of higher-order consciousness from time to time to discuss matters significant for the understanding of primary consciousness. This is the case because the presence of higher-order consciousness allows direct report to an experimenter. As a result, he or she can probe conscious states and their neural correlates with greater assurance. Animals other than humans cannot report their conscious states in the absence of language. Nevertheless, there is ample reason to believe that, on the basis of their behavior and the homologous structures and similar functions of their nervous systems, other animals experience primary consciousness. So the order of study and discussion must, to some extent, proceed from humans "downward." It must never be forgotten, however, that primary consciousness is the fundamental state, for without it, there could be no higher-order consciousness.

Chapter 6

Wider Than the Sky

QUALIA, UNITY, AND COMPLEXITY

By emphasizing the neuroanatomical and dynamic properties of the brain in seeking the mechanisms of consciousness, I may appear to be sidestepping some fundamental issues related to conscious experience. How, for example, does our neural model fit with the experienced properties of a conscious subject? I believe that the issue is best clarified by stressing the neural mechanisms first, and then going back and forth between phenomenal issues and these mechanisms to show their consistency with each other.

One extraordinary phenomenal feature of conscious experience is that normally it is all of a piece—it is unitary. Any experienced conscious moment simultaneously includes sensory input, consequences of motor activity, imagery, emotions, fleeting memories, bodily sensations, and a peripheral fringe. In any ordinary circumstances it does not consist of "just this pencil with which I am writing," nor can I reduce it to that. Yet, at the same time, one unitary scene flows and transforms itself into another complex but also unitary scene. Alternatively, it can shift into diffuse reverie or into high focal attention by choice or under stress.

One way of describing this is to say that while conscious experience is highly integrated, it is at the same time highly differentiated. In short time periods, it can range phenomenally over a multitude of inner states. This apparently unending change and changeability nonetheless cannot at any one time be dissected into unique isolated parts by the person experiencing these subjective states. This is not to deny that consciousness can be modulated by focal attention. We will discuss such focused narrowing of the conscious scene later when we consider the relation between conscious and nonconscious activities.

The subjective experience of rich inner conscious states must be contrasted with the inability of a conscious subject to carry out three or more conscious acts simultaneously—for example, type text, recite a poem, and answer a quiz, all at the same time. This inability to execute multiple tasks simultaneously has caused some to consider consciousness to be of very limited utility. But in fact, it is likely that this apparent limitation derives from the evolutionary necessity that motor actions and plans not be interrupted before completion. Moreover, the view that "chunking" simultaneous conscious acts at best into only two or three units reveals a limit to the efficacy of the conscious state misconstrues the relationship of that state to instrumental acts in the future. As we shall see, a major function of consciousness and its underlying neural mechanisms is planning and rehearsal and, for these, the multifarious complexity of successive inner states is just what is required. For planning, we must rehearse distinctions that make a difference from an individual's vantage point; that is, from the first-person view of a subject. Carrying out motor acts or other performances often requires conscious rehearsal, but, after learning, such acts are more effectively executed by the subject without direct conscious supervision, except when novel circumstances arise. It is not surprising that an attempt to execute two or more of any such acts that require completion is likely to be interrupted by conscious intervention.

How about phenomenal experience itself? What is it that appears to the conscious subject? What does he or she feel? The term "quale" has been applied to the experiencing of feeling—say, of green, or warmth, or pain. Philosophers have considered the understanding of qualia to be a critical problem in consciousness research. Some of their concerns relate to the apparent discrepancy in kind between neural activity and the structure and "feel" of qualia. I shall devote some space to this issue, which, simply stated, explores what it is like to be a conscious individual in a particular species— or, as the philosopher Thomas Nagel has put it, "What is it like to be a bat?"

To get at this issue, a number of subsidiary issues must be addressed. The first relates to the notion that neural activity, as measured and understood by a scientific observer, has none of the properties we ascribe to qualia. Here it is useful to remember that the conscious experience of qualia is a process. The dynamic structural origin of properties, even conscious properties, need not resemble the properties it gives rise to: an explosion does not resemble an explosive. A second issue concerns subjectivity and the first-person perspective. Consciousness is a process that is tied to an individual body and brain and to their history. From an observational point of view, the first-person experience is not written in transferable currency that is completely negotiable by a third-person scientific observer. But it is a reasonable starting point to assume that first-person experiences in individuals of a given species have some things in common. So it is no surprise that, while I can at least surmise as a human what it is like to be you as another human, it is not possible to be nearly as certain in trying to imagine what it is like to be a bat.

I shall indulge later in an exercise to see how our

model of primary consciousness might give rise to a sense of scene even in a bat. But first it is useful to point out that we already have ample evidence from neuroscience to suggest why different qualia have different feels. The neural structures and dynamics underlying vision are distinct from those of smell, and those for touch differ from those of hearing, and so on. Although no scientific description of these pathways and their activities can give rise to a specific quale in the reader's mind, if we assume that he or she has an adequately equipped nervous system, he or she can relate such a description to a first-person experience. No matter what structure underlies a quale, it can be discriminated from others. One might say: "If it weren't this way, it would be that way." The fact that it requires a particular body and a particular brain in a particular environment is no great hindrance to a general analysis of the origin of *different* qualia.

According to the extended TNGS, qualia are high-order discriminations in a complex domain. The experience of a conscious scene as unitary suggests the view that all conscious experiences are qualia. In this view, the separation of qualia into single, narrow feelings such as red, warm, and so forth, while thinkable and verbally describable, does not constitute a full recognition of the discriminations involved. For example, we can, as scientists, describe color experiences in terms of a variety of defining properties, such as the spectral characteristics of the three retinal pigments and the neural responses of a given visual system. We can then plot the various properties of particular experienced colors each as distinct points in a three-dimensional space. But how do we know that the color qualia are in fact what they are, except in the higher-dimensional space that also maps the various other qualia, thus allowing these mutual distinctions? It is in fact the ability to discriminate refined differences of, say, hot and cold in the presence of myriad other qualities such as color in a unitary scene that distinguishes a conscious discrimination from the hot-cold distinction made, for example, by a thermostat. To be conscious is to be able to make such decisions based on multidimensional discriminations or distinctions.

The richness of these differentiable states of consciousness and the unitary nature of each state do not, at first glance, seem compatible. To show that they are compatible, it will suffice to provide a satisfactory account of how the organization of the nervous system can give rise to these properties. These properties are precisely those found in complex systems; therefore I will begin by providing a brief description of some properties of complex systems. A complex system is a system that consists of a variety of smaller parts, each one of which may be functionally segregated. As these heterogeneous parts interact in various combinations, there is a tendency to give rise to system properties that are more integrated. My colleagues and I have described such systems formally. Here, I will give a qualitative account that I believe will serve our purposes. The terms and mathematical *measures* used for characterizing a complex system are borrowed from statistical information theory, but the *premises* of that theory are not accepted by our analysis. Such terms include "independence," "entropy," "mutual information," and "integration." I shall give a few examples of their use, which I believe will clarify their meaning without going into mathematical detail. My goal is to show how a complex system can display integration of its parts but at the same time have many differentiated states combining the properties of these parts.

Let me begin by presenting two extreme examples of systems that are not complex (Figure 8). An ideal gas with particles randomly colliding in elastic collisions is not a complex system. Each particle is independent (it does not stick to the others), and there is no gain or loss of information ("mutual information") exchanged in such a collision. At the other extreme, a perfect crystal is not complex. In the case of such perfect regularity, there is a high degree of integration and mutual information among the units. However, once one knows the so-called space group and the contents of one of the unit cells of which the crystal is composed, no new information is gained in passing to any of the other unit cells.

Now let us consider a complex system. How is it both integrated and differentiated at the same time? We can express the integration of a system in terms of its so-called informational entropy. This is the amount of information it would take to distinguish this system from all possible similar systems made of the same com-

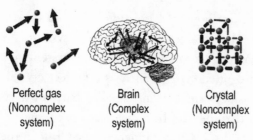

Perfect gas
(Noncomplex
system)

Brain
(Complex
system)

Crystal
(Noncomplex
system)

Figure 8. The contrast between the brain and two hypothetical systems—an ideal gas and a perfect crystal—which have much lower complexity. As a complex system, the brain has small, relatively independent parts that are heterogeneous in structure and function. As they connect by means of various kinds of neuroanatomy, they tend to become integrated across a large number of states generated by the functional connectivity within that anatomy. In the case of the gas, no such integration occurs whereas with the crystal there is high integration but no variety.

ponents, taking into account their relative probabilities of occurrence. Integration is the sum of the entropies of each of the parts of a system minus the entropy of the system as a whole. In the case of an ideal gas, this difference is zero—putting separate bits of the gas together to make a larger volume does not add any new information. But as parts of a system interact and share mutual information (as in a crystal), the entropy of the system is less than the sum of the entropies of its parts, and integration takes on a positive value. In a perfect crystal that value is as high as it can be.

We are now in a position to say in more precise fashion what characterizes a complex system and apply this characterization to the nervous system. Unlike a fully integrated system, such as a perfect crystal, when one considers smaller and smaller parts of a complex system, they deviate from a linear dependence of integration and show more independence. But in the other direction, as larger and larger subsets consisting of such interacting parts are considered, they approach closer to the limit set by a totally integrated system. This is just the property seen in interacting networks of the brain. They exhibit functional segregation (cortical area V1 for orientation, V4 for color, V5 for object motion, and so on) but, through binding via reentry, they become integrated—that is, they exhibit more unitary properties as they are linked together.

We may now apply these ideas to the thalamocortical system in order to reveal a mechanistic neural basis for the unitary yet differentiated properties of a conscious scene or qualia space, the space representing all the different qualia. But before we do, two matters must be considered in addition to what we have said so far. The first is that the thalamocortical system is dynamic. As a result of its enormous numbers of neuronal connections, the reentrant interactions of its excitatory and inhibitory neurons as well as the gating effects of the reticular nucleus and subcortical value systems, the thalamocortical system shows rapid changes in its functional connectivity over fractions of a second. The second matter concerns the relatively large number of internal interactions in that system compared with the number of interactions it has with subcortical systems, such as the basal ganglia, that mediate nonconscious activities of the brain. It appears that the dynamic reentrant thalamocortical system speaks mainly to itself. This defines what we call a functional cluster: most of its neural transactions occur within the thalamus and cortex themselves, and only a relatively few transactions occur with other parts of the brain. As we shall see later, this is an important property that serves to distinguish the neuronal activities subserving consciousness from those that do not.

This functional cluster with its myriad of dynamic reentrant interactions, occurring mainly, but not entirely, in the thalamocortical system, has been called the dynamic core (Figure 9). The dynamic core, with its millisecond-to-millisecond utilization of an extraordinary complex of neural circuits, is precisely the kind of complex neural organization necessary for the unitary yet differentiable properties of the conscious process. It has the reentrant structure capable of integrating or binding the activities of the various thalamic nuclei and the functionally segregated cortical regions to produce a unified scene. Through such interactions, the dynamic core relates value-category memory to perceptual categorization. In addition, it serves to connect conceptual and memory maps to each other. Changes of state in the dynamic core in response to signals from within and without engage new sets of dynamic functionally segregated circuits in short times, and this property accounts for the differentiation of successive scenes constituting the conscious state. Above all, because of the degeneracy and associative properties of its component circuits and neuronal groups, the activity of the core enables conscious animals to carry out high-order discriminations. Qualia *are* these discriminations. The great variety of

---

Figure 9. The dynamic core. The thalamocortical system, which gives rise to the dynamic core, is represented by a fine meshwork of cortical and thalamic areas and reentrant connections. The core is composed of a functional cluster that speaks mainly to itself through an enormous complex of signals that fluctuate in time across the reentrant meshwork. Responses triggered by the reentrant dynamic core can also stimulate nonconscious responses. These travel along parallel, polysynaptic, one-directional pathways that leave the cortex, reach the various components of the basal ganglia and certain thalamic nuclei, and finally return to the cortex (as in Figure 3, middle diagram). In this way, responses subserving consciousness can connect to activity patterns in nonconscious areas, served mainly but not exclusively by the basal ganglia. The ganglia and the thalamus have been displaced and enlarged for clarity. Areas of the cortex not in the core at some particular time can also interact with such nonconscious activity patterns. At some subsequent time hundreds of milliseconds later, however, neuronal groups from these areas can participate in the core.

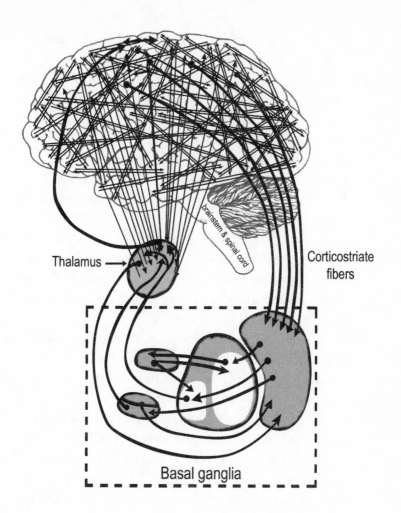

Thalamus

brainstem & spinal cord

Corticostriate fibers

Basal ganglia

discriminations emerges because the dynamic core is a complex system that can maintain functionally segregated parts while integrating the activity of these parts over time in a very rich combinatorial fashion. Each transient set of degenerate core circuits may underlie a scene, to be replaced in short time periods by another set, yielding a changed scene. Of course, this whole picture is consonant with the TNGS and its notion of the brain as a selectional system, one reflecting both constancy and variation.

In a developed individual, the range of integrations over the entire qualia space can be enlarged by experience or dynamically diminished by attention. Both processes are important in conscious planning. Think, for example, of the subtle changes that occur in an oenophile after more and more refined discussions during multiple tastings of various categories of wine. But how can such differential discriminations be made by just that one person, that single self? Can the workings of the reentrant dynamic core account for the fact that the conscious scene belongs to a subjective self?

We will consider this at length when we discuss higher-order consciousness. Here I can provide a short account of the changes that are likely to occur during development and early experience. The earliest discriminations of consciousness must concern perceptual categorizations related to the body itself. These are mediated through signals from structures in the brainstem and in various value systems that map the state of the body (see

Figure 7). As I mentioned before, the signals from these "self" systems report the relation of the body to both the inside and the outside environments. Such signals include so-called proprioceptive, kinesthetic or somato-sensory, and autonomic components. These components, which signal, respectively, the position of the body, the action of muscles and joints, and the regulation of the internal environment, affect almost every aspect of our being. They regulate bodily functions of which we, as mature individuals, are only dimly aware. Like the value systems that signal the salience of various internal and external events, these components are at the deep center of conscious experience. The early bodily-based consciousness of self (reinforced even by early fetal movements) is likely to provide the initial guidelines of our qualia space, out of which all subsequent memories, based on signals from the world ("nonself"), are elaborated. Thus, even before higher-order consciousness appears, a bodily-based neural reference space or body-centered scene will be built up. An animal or a newborn baby will experience a scene in reference to a self but will have no nameable self that is differentiable from within. Such a nameable self emerges in humans as higher-order consciousness develops during the elaboration of semantic and linguistic capabilities and social interactions. Qualia can then be named and explicitly distinguished. But even before that, qualia are already discernible and almost certainly referenced to the ongoing categorization of the self by primary consciousness. In the complex system underlying such consciousness, there are already hosts of qualia that consist of all the conscious states that can be discriminated. The dynamic core, whose activities are enriched through learning, continues throughout life to be influenced by new processes of categorization connected to what might be termed the bodily self. It is important to understand, however, that the functional cluster comprising the core should *not* be identified at any one time with *all* of the cortex or thalamus, parts of which are continually interacting with nonconscious regions of the brain.

There remains the question of how the self is actually aware of an ongoing scene. We must confront the difference between the first-person experience and the third-person description of the neural substate that underlies that experience. Perhaps it may be useful to imagine a demon or homunculoid observer whose task is to confront what it is like to have that experience by interpreting the metastable core states. Imagine that such an observer is present in the brain and able to witness and mathematically interpret the myriad neural workings of value-category memory in the dynamic core of a conscious individual in a given animal species. Such a memory system is already based on species-specific categories related to past perceptual experience. Now also imagine that self-categories are at the forefront, even though they are mixed with those perceptual categories that are related to nonself. As ongoing activities of the reentrant dynamic core lead to the creation of a new scene, our homunculoid can witness the neural activity responsible for creating that scene and also notice that the "self," dynamically and continually constructed from bodily cues, can also be related to that scene. Even with those capabilities, however, this imaginary homunculoid does not and cannot perceive or control the high-level discriminations that underlie the conscious activities of the individual in question. Nor can such a demon experience the qualia that accompany these activities.

This somewhat bizarre construction suggests that even with his analytical skills, the homunculoid could never come to know what it is like to be a conscious human. We inserted him into the brain and gave him the capacity to read the core in an attempt to understand the privileged nature of conscious experience. Observations from without, or even from within, by a demon that does not have the animal's body cannot fully recapture the content of that privacy. But observing how categorical memory referred to self can deal with new categories to make a scene may be heuristically useful in imagining how the gap between subjective awareness and neural action can be bridged. The homunculoid, of course, does not exist. Indeed, the very imagining of such a construct forces us to confront a central issue. This issue concerns the causal efficacy of consciousness, to which we now turn.

Chapter 9

Consciousness and Causation

THE PHENOMENAL TRANSFORM

e now come to the crux of our theory of consciousness. At this point in our account, we must confront two questions, introduced earlier, both related to causation. The first is: How is the conscious process entailed by neural processes? We have in a sense already answered this question, but the answer must be reformulated to confront the second question, which is: Is consciousness itself causal?

Our previous account suggested that conscious processes arise from the enormous numbers of reentrant interactions between value-category memory systems that are largely present in the more anterior parts of the thalamocortical system and the more posterior systems that carry out perceptual categorization. Through the complex shifting states of the dynamic core, these interactions underlie the unitary property of conscious states, as well as the shifting diversity of these states over time. Because the earliest interactions involve bodily inputs from centers of the brain concerned with value systems, motor areas, and regions involved in emotional responses, the core processes are always centered around a self that serves as a reference for memory. In primary consciousness, this self exists in a remembered present, reflecting the integration of a scene around a small interval of time present. While an animal having this primary consciousness has a long-term memory of past events, it has no extensive ability to deal explicitly with the concept of a past or a future. Nevertheless, it can carry out a vast number of conscious discriminations, discriminations that are experienced as qualia. Only with the evolution of higher-order consciousness based on semantic capabilities do explicit concepts of self, of past, and of future emerge.

This account implies that the fundamental neural activity of the reentrant dynamic core converts the signals from the world and the brain into a "phenomenal transform"—into what it is like to be that conscious animal, to have its qualia. The existence of such a transform (our experience of qualia) reflects the ability to make high-order distinctions or discriminations that would not be possible without the neural activity of the core. Our thesis has been that the phenomenal transform, the set of discriminations, is entailed by that neural activity. It is not caused by that activity but it is, rather, a simultaneous property of that activity.

This brings us directly to the second question. Is the phenomenal transform itself causal? This question is pivotal, not only in considering how conscious acts occur but also in addressing whether consciousness arose in evolution as an efficacious or adaptive process. To explore this issue in a direct fashion, let us call the phenomenal transform and its processes C. Call the underlying neural core processes C'. Both C and C' could be indexed (C'_0, C_0; C'_1, C_1; C'_2, C_2; C'_3, C_3; and so forth) to indicate their successive states in time, but for now let us consider them without addressing the temporal issue. We have pointed out that C is a process, not a thing, that it reflects higher-order discriminations, and that it does not occur in the absence of C'. But, given the laws of physics, C itself cannot be causal; it reflects a relationship and cannot exert a physical force either directly or through field properties. It is entailed by C', however, and the detailed discriminatory activity of C' *is* causal.

That is, although C accompanies C', it is C' that is causal of other neural events and certain bodily actions. The world is causally closed—no spooks or spirits

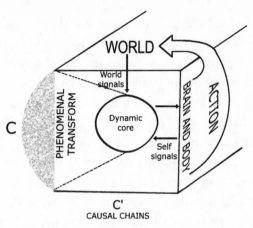

Figure 10. Causal chains in the world, body, and brain affect the reentrant dynamic core. Core activities (C′) in turn affect further neural events and actions. Core processes confer the ability to make high-order distinctions. The entailed phenomenal transform (C) with its qualia consists of those distinctions.

are present—and occurrences in the world can only respond to the neural events constituting C′ (Figure 10).

Consciousness C as a property of C′ is a reflection of the capacity to make refined discriminations in a multidimensional qualia space. This phenomenal transform, reflecting events in that space, is a reliable indicator of the underlying causal C′ events. The consequence of this line of reasoning is that evolution selected C′ (underlain by the neural activities of the dynamic core) for the efficacy in planning conferred by its activity. At the same time, however, such C′ activity entailed corresponding C states. Indeed, there is no other way for an individual animal to directly experience the effects of C′. The phenomenal transform provides an integrated scene that reflects discriminations made possible by C′ activity and thus provides a coherent and reliable indicator to the individual of the causal states underlying his consciousness.

This entailment of C by C′ also provides a cogent means for communication of C′ states to other individuals. Even that communication has C′ as its causal vehicle. The relationship of entailment between C and C′ implies that the so-called zombie argument of philosophers is logically impossible. That argument asserts that a zombie (an individual having C′ but without a phenomenal transform C) could carry out operations identical to those of an individual with C. So, for example, without feelings, qualia, emotions, or a scene, a zombie art critic could, according to the argument, make identical judgments about the superiority of one painting over another to those made by a human art critic putting forth the same judgments while experiencing C. The argument we are making here implies, however, that if C′ did not entail C, it could *not* have identical effects. The zombie would not know what it is like to be a conscious human and could not carry out the necessary discriminations in a fashion identical to a human. Moreover, being nonconscious, it could not be conscious of being conscious. To have C′ as a result of core activities is to have C as a reliable property.

How might the C′–C relationship have evolved?

I have already considered the necessary development of reentrant connections between brain regions carrying out perceptual categorization and value-category memory. Here I want briefly to speculate on the origin of the relationship of entailment between C' and C. It is reasonable to assume that the development of the ability to carry out refined distinctions conferred by the dynamic core would have selective advantage. The core could conceivably have evolved even in species without extensive communicative abilities. I find it more attractive, however, to consider that, in animal species in which rich communication of emotional states led to enhanced fitness, it would have been advantageous to connect the ability (C') to make refined distinctions with the communication of these distinctions. Animals so evolved would communicate efficacious C' states in terms of C. C, after all, is the only information available that reflects C' states to each animal and to others. As long as C states reflect C' states reliably, the fact that the world is causally closed and that only C' is causal would not undermine the role of C as a vehicle of communication.

The fact that the world is causally closed has been noted by certain philosophers of mind, notably Jaegwon Kim. Following another philosopher, Donald Davidson, Kim has proposed that a C state as a psychological state is "supervenient," or dependent on a physical state (in our terms, C') that is causal. In early work, he has described all causal relations involving psychological events as epiphenomenal supervenient causal relations. Presumably this refers to C′ as causal since "epiphenomenal" means causally impotent. Although these notions are roughly in accord with our account, I would not designate any mental event as directly causal, for it is a relationship and cannot exert a physical force. But the neural firings in C′ can do so, for example, by activating muscles. By providing a description of how C depends on C′ in a specific neural model we can go beyond an abstract statement about the dependence of C on C′.

In general, I have been in accord with, and even inspired by, the views of William James on consciousness. But I do differ from him in interpreting the relationship between consciousness and causality. In *The Principles of Psychology,* James quotes T. H. Huxley, Darwin's bulldog:

> The consciousness of brutes would appear to be related to the mechanism of their body simply as a collateral product of its working, and to be as completely without any power of modifying that working as the steam-whistle which accompanies the work of a locomotive engine is without influence on machinery. Their volition, if they have any, is an emotion *indicative* of physical changes, not a *cause* of such changes . . . to the best of my judgement, the argumentation which applies to brutes holds equally good of men; and, therefore, that all states of consciousness in us, as in them,

are immediately caused by molecular changes of the brain-substance. It seems to me that in men, as in brutes, there is no proof that any state of consciousness is the cause of change in the motion of the matter of the organism. If these positions are well based, it follows that our mental conditions are simply the symbols in consciousness of the changes which take place automatically in the organisms; and that, to take an extreme illustration, the feeling we call volition is not the cause of a voluntary act, but the symbol of that state of the brain which is the immediate cause of that act. We are conscious automata.

James takes issue with this view, which he calls the "Automaton-Theory." He grasps its import and even adds his own metaphors, saying: "So the melody floats from the harp-string, but neither checks nor quickens its vibration; so the shadow runs alongside the pedestrian, but in no way influences his steps." Then he mounts a counterargument, insisting that the particulars of the distribution of consciousness point to its being efficacious. His argument rests on three legs. First, he argues that consciousness is a selecting agency. Next he argues that the cerebral cortex is inherently unstable and that this apparent defect can be corrected by consciousness, which stabilizes the cortex by being a "fighter for ends," reinforcing activity favorable for the organism and repressing unfavorable activity. Third, James argues from the fact that pleasures are associated with beneficial experiences and pains with detrimental ones. If pleasure and pains had no efficacy, he did not see why the reverse (pain, beneficial; pleasure, detrimental) could not be true were the automaton theory to be correct. Consciousness, it seemed to James, is added in evolution "for the sake of steering a nervous system grown too complex to regulate itself." James was too honest a partisan not to point out an essential mystery entailed by his position: "*How* such reaction of the consciousness upon the [nerve] currents may occur must remain at present unsolved." It is noteworthy that, more recently, another gifted scientist, Roger Sperry, has taken the position that consciousness can actually affect neuronal firing.

Obviously, I have taken a contrary position: Nothing prevents us from espousing the view that all of the points made by James can be answered by the appropriate evolution of C′ states along with their corresponding C states. Provided that a suitable mechanism of consciousness—that it arises from the activity of the reentrant dynamic core—is provided, there is no problem concerning effects on "nerve currents."

If I disagree with James, I must also take issue with Huxley: we are not automata. The TNGS, with its firm grounding in population and selectionist thinking, rejects the notion that we are machines or, more precisely, that we are Turing machines. Indeed, the variability of consciousness, which arises from the nature of the dynamic core, is not a defect. This is so because the variability is accompanied by integrative activity and selection. The very richness of core states provides the grounds for new matches to the vicissitudes of the environment. Those matches are stabilized through the workings of the brain as a complex system.

What is unusual about the position we are taking is not that C is an epiphenomenon or, if it is, that it poses a paradox. In fact, it does not. The unusual aspect of our view of causation is that C states, even while not directly causal, reliably reflect the incredibly refined discriminatory capacity of C′ states. C states or qualia are the discriminations entailed by C′ states. This is the basic feature of the conscious activity that results from the reentrant interactions of the dynamic core.

The tight relationship of entailment between C′ and C necessarily involves a first-person experience. Any alternative third-person assessment of C′ consequences (as with our homunculoid) would require an extraordinarily rapid mathematical synthesis of an individual's immediate core state, and a means for connecting this synthesis of extraordinarily complex events to subsequent events in the core. Clearly, evolution, powerful as it is, could not assure such capabilities. Moreover, to allow an effective measure of causal consequences, such capabilities would also require a more or less complete knowledge of each individual's prior value-category history. Given the existence of novelty and the selectional nature of neural events, a synthesis of this type could not be carried out by a computer, no matter how powerful. Even our bizarre homunculoid could not *experience* the processes we presumed it could follow.

When talking to each other as if our C states are causal, we do not have to be concerned about the particular C' state that is the true cause of our exchange. The relation of entailment that makes C a property of C' is an accurate track of the relationship of C' to causal efficacy. Although at first glance it may seem somewhat eerie that all of our transactions, first- and third-person, rely on neural events, there is in fact no contradiction implied. The only contradictions that might arise derive from the contrary assumptions: that C' states can lead to identical effects without entailing C, that C can exist without C', or that C is itself causal.

The phenomenal transform is an elegant means of conveying the integrated states of C' on a first-person basis. There is no other way to directly experience these neural events. Even in the interchange between two conscious humans, the phenomenal transform provides an indicator of causal relations without being causal itself. The subjective state reflects the ongoing properties of the neural states of the core. It is qualia space itself— consciousness in all its richness.

Chapter 8

The Conscious and the Nonconscious

AUTOMATICITY AND ATTENTION

We are all familiar with habit and with automatic activities, such as riding a bike, based on previous conscious acts of learning. We are also familiar with the various levels of our conscious attentive acts. These range from a kind of free-floating "rest state" of diffuse attention and awareness to highly focal attention to one idea, image, or thought. All of these phenomena are related in one way or another to the functioning of subcortical structures that collaborate with the dynamic thalamocortical core. These subcortical structures—the basal ganglia, the cerebellum, and the hippocampus—were described earlier. I have called these the organs of succession because of their relation to movement and time.

There is no doubt that the basal ganglia and cerebellum are important in the initiation and control of movement. As I have already mentioned, the hippocampus is concerned with the conversion of short-term memory into long-term memory by interacting with the cerebral cortex. After the bilateral removal of the hippocampal formation, episodic memory can no longer be established, although all episodic memories previous to the lesion remain intact.

In considering automaticity and attention, I shall focus mainly on the transactions between the basal ganglia and the cerebral cortex. These transactions connect nonconscious functions to conscious ones. To reveal those transactions, I must make another excursion into neuroanatomy. This excursion, which requires consideration of a small thicket of Latin names, will reveal strong differences between the organization of the thalamocortical core and the system of basal ganglia (see Figure 3). But the names are not as important as the anatomical connections to which they give rise.

The basal ganglia are five deep nuclei that are at the center of the brain (Figure 11). They receive connections from the cerebral cortex and then send projections to the cortex by way of the thalamus. Their connections to the cortex are topographically organized (that is, like a map) in both directions. They also connect to each other in a series of polysynaptic loops.

A major portion of the basal ganglia, constituting *input nuclei* from the cortex, is the so-called striatum, which consists of the caudate nucleus and putamen. The remaining nuclei are the globus pallidus, the substantia nigra, and the subthalamic nucleus. The globus pallidus and one part of the substantia nigra make up the major *output nuclei* projecting to the thalamus. Their output may be looked upon in turn as the input to the dynamic thalamocortical core. In addition to the input to the striatum by the cerebral cortex, the intralaminar nuclei of the thalamus also project to the striatum. It is particularly important to note that the basal ganglia receive inputs from practically all regions of the cortex. This is in sharp contrast to the cerebellum, which gets input from a more restricted sensorimotor portion of the cortex. While the cerebellum links to the motor and premotor regions of the cortex, the basal ganglia project as well to the prefrontal cortex and to the so-called association areas, the activity of which helps to weigh decisions related to action.

According to classical accounts, there are two main circuits through which the basal ganglia exert their effects. We can best describe the effects of the basal ganglia by considering only motor activities for now; the same mechanisms apply to the other circuits engaged by the ganglia. The so-called direct pathway receives excitatory (glutamatergic) inputs from the cortex to the striatum. The striatum then projects to the internal segment of the globus pallidus and to the so-called pars reticulata of the substantia nigra. Both of these project in turn to the thalamus and then back to the cortex. The indirect pathway follows a different route. It goes from the striatum to the external segment of the globus pallidus, which then sends fibers on to the subthalamic nucleus. This nucleus then projects back to the pallidus and substantia nigra.

The outputs from the striatum are inhibitory. Excitation of striatal neurons by the cortex inhibits the in-

---

Figure 11. The motor circuit of the basal ganglia, illustrating the polysynaptic loops carrying inhibitory and disinhibitory signals via the thalamus. This circuit of the basal ganglia is a subcortical feedback loop from the motor and somatosensory areas of the cortex, traveling through segregated portions of the basal ganglia and thalamus, and thence back to the premotor cortex, the supplementary motor area, and the motor cortex. (The basal ganglia and thalamus have been displaced and enlarged for clarity.)

The basal ganglia are involved in regulating motor programs and plans and also appear to be concerned with various aspects of attention. This diagram does not show the more extensive and similarly organized projections of the basal ganglia to other brain areas, such as parts of the forebrain (frontal and parietal cortex), that are particularly important for attention.

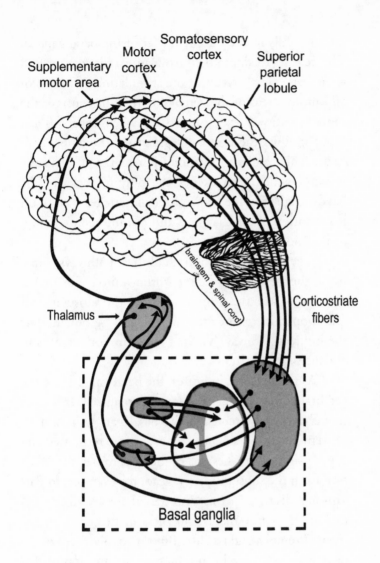

Supplementary motor area

Motor cortex

Somatosensory cortex

Superior parietal lobule

brainstem & spinal cord

Corticostriate fibers

Thalamus

Basal ganglia

hibitory cells in the output nuclei of the basal ganglia. This releases (disinhibits) the thalamic cells and can lead to movement as a result of the stimulation of premotor and motor areas of the cerebral cortex. In contrast, the indirect pathway exerts its effects when corticostriatal input inhibits the external segment of the globus pallidus. This results in disinhibition of the subthalamic nucleus, which then excites the output nuclei of the basal ganglia via the transmitter glutamate. The result is inhibition of the thalamus and diminished excitation of the motor areas.

A key modulation of both of these pathways comes from the action of the neurotransmitter dopamine, which mediates the projections from the substantia nigra. Dopamine excites the direct pathway but inhibits the indirect pathway. The net result in both cases is to enhance movement.

As this account indicates, the basal ganglia and the cerebral cortex are very differently organized. It is clear that the motor circuits of the basal ganglia modulate movement by enhancing some cortical responses and suppressing others. Lesions of the dopaminergic projection from the substantia nigra lead, for example, to Parkinson's disease. In this disorder, there are difficulties in initiating movements, slowness in executing movements, tremors, and rigidity. But the involvement of the basal ganglia in carrying out motor programs is probably not the only effect these nuclei have on cortical functioning. There is evidence that patients with Parkinson's disease can have cognitive defects and overall slowing of thought. There is also evidence that the basal ganglia are involved in defects and repetitive actions connected with obsessive-compulsive disorders. Moreover, in hereditary Huntington's disease, resulting from loss of cholinergic cells and GABAergic cells in the striatum, there are severe cognitive defects. These include absentmindedness and, finally, dementia accompanied by severe movement disorders. These severe cognitive defects are probably related to the effects of the disease on the projections of the basal ganglia to the prefrontal cortex.

A series of observations obtained by brain scanning techniques is consistent with the hypothesis that the connections between basal ganglia and cortex are involved in the execution of automatic motor programs. During conscious learning of tasks, a considerable amount of the cerebral cortex is engaged. With practice, conscious attention is not required, and acts become automatic, as, for example, after learning to ride a bicycle. At such a point, brain scans show much less involvement of the cortex unless novelty is introduced, requiring further conscious attention. It is an attractive hypothesis that collaborations between the cortex and basal ganglia set up the synaptic changes that lie behind such procedural learning. So, for example, practicing musical passages will eventually result in the ability to "rattle them off" without detailed attention. Later, two such learned passages may be joined by conscious efforts and further practice, again to become automatic in execution. While performing, a pianist playing a concerto with an orchestra may execute passages without conscious attention, note by note, but simultaneously may plan consciously or think ahead about an upcoming musical phrase or tempo. The nonconscious portion of this execution is, by our hypothesis, governed largely by interactions between the basal ganglia and the parts of the cortex not engaged in core activities.

The implication of this hypothesis is that certain portions of the cortex may be engaged in these interactions without being directly involved in the operation of the dynamic core. But when necessary, input and output from the core can invoke learned responses involving those portions of cortex and basal ganglia, routines that were previously nonconscious.

In such interactions, attention can become involved to varying degrees, and it is likely that conscious attention is mediated by more than one mechanism. For example, in a "free-floating" or "rest" state of consciousness with little focal attention, it is reasonable to expect that corticocortical reentry and shifting thalamocortical reentry would provide sufficient bases. In more focal, but not highly exclusive, states of attention, gating by the reticular nucleus of the specific nuclei of the thalamus might come into play and restrict core activity. And in highly focal attentive states, a reasonable surmise is that the loops of interaction between the basal ganglia and the frontal and parietal cortices engaged in the core may provide a central mechanism. This hypothesis assumes that motor components of attention play an essential and even controlling role in imagined acts, but without engaging actual movements. The basal ganglion circuitry is well suited for this. Unlike the circuitry of the cerebellum, it has no direct output connections to the brainstem and spinal cord, but is connected to large amounts of the cortex through the thalamus.

By this means, during highly focal attention, perceptual-motor loops and global mappings may serve to limit dynamic core states to the target of conscious attention. In this condition, it is as if the attending subject is unconscious of all but the attended task. The inhibitory loops of basal ganglion circuits and the ability to modulate inhibition by balances between the direct and indirect pathways would seem to be well adapted to this mechanism.

The hypotheses put forth here are based on the notion that the complex reentrant dynamics of the thalamocortical core can be influenced by nonconscious brain activity. I have not dealt with the Freudian unconscious and the notion of repression, which remains to some extent a vexed subject. But it is conceivable that the modulation of value systems could provide a basis for the selective inhibition of pathways related to particular memories. For now, it is sufficient for my purposes to deal with the interaction between conscious states and those which are necessarily nonconscious.

The anatomical excursions in this chapter were necessary to reveal the differences between nonconscious structures like the basal ganglia and cerebellum and the thalamocortical arrangements of the core. Core elements are enormously reentrant. In contrast, basal ganglion elements are in long inhibitory loops. While the loci of interaction of such loops are richly distributed, in the main, the complexity of the dynamic core is far greater than that of the polysynaptic loops of the ganglia. As I pointed out before, the core acts as a functional cluster, interacting largely with itself to yield conscious states. The ability to open up or restrict cortical–basal ganglion interactions, thus modulating the content of consciousness, can nevertheless affect the range of the core cluster and alter attentional states.

Chapter 9

Higher-Order Consciousness and Representation

My account so far has been focused mainly on primary consciousness. As far as we are aware, animals with only primary consciousness lack a sense of the past, a concept of the future, and a socially defined and nameable self. Moreover, they are not conscious of being conscious. Lacking these functions does not mean that they lack a self, that they lack imagery in the remembered present, or that they do not have long-term memory. Within the attentive focus of consciousness in the remembered present, they can even carry out plans and react in terms of their past value-category memory.

So what is missing? According to the extended TNGS, they have no semantic capabilities. They are not able to use symbols as tokens to lend meaning to acts and events and to reason about events not unfolding in the present moment. This does not mean that to have higher-order consciousness an animal needs to have a language. There is some evidence that such primates as chimpanzees have semantic abilities, but little or no syntactical ability, and thus that they lack true language. There is, nevertheless, evidence that they are able to recognize mirror images of themselves and to reason about the consequences of the actions of other chimpanzees or of humans. Given this and their semantic capabilities, it is likely that they have a form of higher-order consciousness.

Our main reference species for higher-order consciousness is ourselves. We not only have biological individuality but, in addition to having a self acting in the remembered present, we have higher-order consciousness and a socially and linguistically defined self. We are conscious of being conscious, have explicit narrative awareness of the past, and can construct scenarios in an imagined future. We have a true language because we have syntactic capabilities in addition to our phonetic and semantic capabilities. Given the acquisition and accumulation of a lexicon, humans can use verbal tokens and symbols to divorce themselves from the remembered present by acts of attention. Of course, for higher-order consciousness to operate, primary consciousness is still necessary, even if its immediate claims are temporarily displaced by such acts of attention.

A number of interesting questions are prompted by these observations. One is related to the functioning of the hippocampus. This neural structure is necessary for episodic memory, the long-term memory of sequential events, the brain's "narrative." As I have mentioned before, it is known that extirpation of the hippocampus bilaterally in adults eliminates the transformation of short-term consciousness and memory into long-term memories of experience. After bilateral hippocampal removal, a patient retains episodic memories and narrative capabilities for events up to the time of the removal. But after the operation, he or she cannot recall a sequence of experiences except for very short time periods. It is not known whether being born without the hippocampus bilaterally would mean that an individual would lack consciousness. But I would conjecture that, even if some form of primary consciousness were retained, it is likely that higher-order consciousness would not develop. Higher-order consciousness rests in part on episodic memory, and in the absence of such memory coherent semantic activity would not be likely to develop.

The origin first of semantic abilities and then of syntactic abilities during evolution is a matter of debate. It is certainly simplistic to suggest that linguistic abilities emerged only with of the development of Broca's and

Wernicke's areas of the cerebral cortex. When these areas in the cortex are damaged, it can lead to various forms of the linguistic impairment known as aphasia. Novel subcortical structures, as well as the expansion of the prefrontal cortex, were also likely to have been involved in the evolution of regions making grammar and therefore true language possible. Whatever the case, it seems likely that new reentrant pathways and circuits appeared among these brain regions as a key basis for the evolutionary emergence of semantic and, finally, linguistic ability during evolution. The appearance of such pathways is thus critical for the development of higher-order consciousness (Figure 12).

As these capabilities develop in an individual, the range of conscious thought expands greatly. The brain is capable of going beyond the information given, as the psychologist Jerome Bruner puts it. Reentrant interactions between maps mediating concepts, those mediating linguistic tokens, and the nonconscious portions of the brain make it possible for consciousness to exploit memory, even in the absence of new perceptual information. It must not be imagined, however, that linguistic performance will immediately guarantee the full capabilities of higher-order consciousness. During childhood, increasing competence must develop and be coordinated with conceptual and memory systems before the full flowering of higher-order consciousness.

Anthropologists have speculated about the development of language in hominines. Surely one cannot

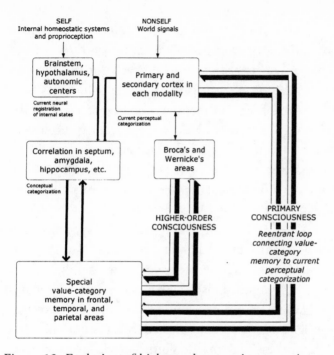

Figure 12. Evolution of higher-order consciousness. A new reentrant loop appears in primates with semantic capabilities and expands greatly during the evolution of hominines with the emergence of language. The acquisition of a new kind of memory, exploiting semantic capabilities and ultimately true language with syntax leads to a conceptual explosion. As a result, higher-order consciousness appears and concepts of the self, the past, and the future become connected to primary consciousness. Consciousness of consciousness becomes possible. (See Figure 7 to relate this scheme to that for primary consciousness.)

ignore the development of the vocal tract and space above the larynx for speech, the motor regulation of respiration during speech, and the bases for the auditory discrimination of coarticulated sounds. Much has been made also of the enormous and evolutionarily rapid development of the cerebral cortex in human evolution. The adoption of bipedal posture was almost certainly a necessary prerequisite for cortical enlargement, as it lifted constraints on craniofacial morphology, thus providing accommodation for a large cortex.

One wonders whether, in addition, bipedalism also allowed complete freedom of the forelimbs so that gestures assumed increased communicative significance. In some deaf populations and certain deaf-mute individuals, gestural communication without the syntax of true sign language has been observed. Such communication by mime suggests that linguistic precursors may have included gesturing as well as vocal signs. In freeing the upper extremities from brachiation (climbing or hanging) or walking, a whole precursor set involving the interpretation of gestures by the self and by others may have been opened up for early hominines. Whether infants who have learned to walk, and have their upper limbs free, develop similar capabilities before the exercise of extensive speech acts is a question that remains. The acquisition of language may be enormously facilitated by the development of conscious imagery related to movements and motor control. Almost certainly, concepts of objects, events, and succession must exist in a child's mind before the exercise of language. According to these ideas, the sequences of actions of the free upper extremities may prepare the basal ganglion–cortical loops for the emergence of syntactical sequences, establishing what might be called a protosyntax.

Clearly, one of the largest steps toward the acquisition of true language is the realization that an arbitrary token—a gesture or a word—stands for a thing or an event. When a sufficiently large lexicon of such tokens is subsequently accumulated, higher-order consciousness can greatly expand in range. Associations can be made by metaphor, and with ongoing activity, early metaphor can be transformed into more precise categories of intrapersonal and interpersonal experience. The gift of narrative and an expanded sense of temporal succession then follow. While the remembered present is, in fact, a reflection of true physical time, higher-order consciousness makes it possible to relate a socially constructed self to past recollections and future imaginations. The Heraclitean illusion of a point in the present moving from the past into the future is constructed by these means. This illusion, mixed with the sense of a narrative and metaphorical ability, elevates higher-order consciousness to new heights. Consideration of these capacities turns our attention to the issue of representation "in the mind."

Modern cognitive science rests heavily on notions of mental representation and, in some sectors, on the notion that the brain carries out "computations." To a certain extent, neuroscientists tend to use the terms "representation" or "encoding" somewhat differently to refer to the correlation or covariance of patterns of neural firings with perceptual inputs or memory states. Unless a distinction is made about the role of consciousness in applying these terms, confusion can result.

As a term, "representation" has had a very liberal usage—it has been applied to images, gestures, language, and so on. In most cases, reference and meaning are attached to its use. But it is a common error to equate meaning and mental representation, for reasons that I shall consider in due course. In any event, it is difficult to avoid the conclusion that consciousness and representation are intimately related. While it is possible for a neurophysiologist to say that a pattern of firing that is correlated with an input signal is a representation, this usage reflects a third-person point of view. As such, it does not encompass mental imagery, concepts, and thoughts, and certainly not the freight of intentionality—that is, beliefs, desires, and intentions.

The position I shall take here is that, although the conscious process involves representation, the neural substrate of consciousness is nonrepresentational. This has the corollary that forms of representation occur in C, but do not compel the underlying C′ states (see figure 10). In this view, memory is nonrepresentational and concepts are the outcome of the brain mapping its own perceptual maps leading to generalities or "universals." While memory and concepts are, together with value systems, necessary for meaning or semantic content, they are not identical to that content.

The advantage of this position is that it does not tie the questions of meaning and reference to a one-to-one correspondence with either brain states or environmental states. At the same time, the enormous varieties of "representations" can be accounted for in terms of states of primary and higher-order consciousness. For example, mental images arise in a primary-conscious scene largely by the same neural processes by which direct perceptual images arise. One relies on memory, the other on signals from without. Concepts, on the other hand, need not rest on imagery but rather depend on global mappings and certain activities of motor systems, which need not necessarily engage the motor cortex, and therefore do not lead to movement. At a higher level, cognition and intentionality are simply parts of the conscious process that may or may not entail imagery.

This view rejects the notion of computation and the idea that there is a "language of thought." Meaning is not identical to "mental representation." Instead, it arises as a result of the play between value systems, varying environmental cues, learning, and nonrepresentational memory. By its very nature, the conscious process embeds representation in a degenerate, context-dependent web: there are many ways in which individual neural circuits, synaptic populations, varying environmental signals, and previous history can lead to the same meaning.

The problem of representation and intentionality

is related to the problem of explaining how higher-order consciousness itself arises. The essential issue to grasp is that the reentrant circuitry underlying consciousness is enormously degenerate. There is no single circuit activity or code that corresponds to a given conscious "representation." A neuron may contribute to that "representation" at one moment, and in the next have no contribution to make. The same is true of context-dependent interactions with the environment. A shift of context can change the qualia that are parts of a representation, or even recompose some qualia and still keep that representation. In any event, there are other aspects of qualia related to sensation that are not included in any representation.

The relationships to the processes of integration and differentiation in the complex dynamic core underlying consciousness follow directly from these notions. Core states themselves do not "represent" a given image, concept, or scene in a one-to-one fashion. Instead, depending on input, environment, body state, and other contexts, different core states can underlie a particular representation. The interactions are relational and have the properties of polymorphous sets. These are sets, like Ludwig Wittgenstein's "games," that are defined neither by singly necessary nor by jointly sufficient conditions. If, for example, there are n different criteria for games today, *any* subset m of criteria, where m is much smaller than n, may suffice to define a game or, in the case at hand, a subset of core states underlying a particular representation.

While this view does not have the crisp properties of logical atomism or of computer models of the mind, it is in accord with a number of observations on language and reference. By pointing out that, for any representation, there can be many underlying neural states and context-dependent signals, it takes account of the historical nature of conscious experience. Above all, it is in accord with the enormous complexity of the relations underlying any given "representation." The problem of explaining the enormous variety of representations can be resolved by considering how relations arise among the variety of conscious states and, above all, among their enormously complex neural correlates in the core.

So far, I have said little about experiments designed to reveal the neural correlates of consciousness. The complexities of representation provide an opportunity to discuss briefly one experiment of this kind. It was designed to ask what happens when a person becomes aware of a perceptual object. The results show that each individual's brain shows widespread reentrant interactions when that subject becomes aware of an object. The data also show that different individuals reporting similar conscious responses have different individual patterns—that is, each case is distinct from the others.

The experiment employs a noninvasive technique called magnetoencephalography, which measures minute electrical currents that occur within as few as ten thousand neurons by detecting the magnetic fields associated with these currents. It does this by using special devices that rely on superconductivity, the conductance of electricity essentially without resistance at very low temperatures. In one version of the apparatus, 148 of these superconducting devices are distributed in a helmet over the living subject's head. The measurement of fields is carried out in a shielded room to minimize outside interference.

The actual experiment relies on a phenomenon known as binocular rivalry. The subject, wearing glasses with one red lens and one blue lens, stares at a screen displaying vertical red bars crossed at right angles by horizontal blue bars. As constructive as the eye and the brain are, these disparate images cannot be reconciled or fused into one. Instead, the subject first sees vertical red bars and then, perhaps a few seconds later, sees horizontal blue bars. So it goes alternately; each time red is seen the subject presses a right-hand switch, and each time blue is seen the subject presses a left-hand switch. The switch responses are recorded simultaneously with the magnetic responses of the brain.

The data are treated by mathematical techniques that eventually yield plots of the magnetic intensity over specific areas of the cerebral cortex when the subject reports consciousness of the object and also when no such report is given. (Remember that the brain "sees" the red verticals and blue horizontals whether the subject reports being conscious of them or not.) Another mathematical technique can be used to measure whether neuronal groups in distant parts of the brain fire synchronously or not, thus testing for the appearance of reentry.

The results are remarkable. When the subject is not conscious of any bars, the brain nonetheless responds in a swath going from the visual areas in the posterior parts of the cortex to the frontal areas related to so-called higher functions. But when the subject reports being conscious of red or blue bars, the responses show very specific patterns. Some brain areas show decreases in the intensity of their activity, while, in others, activity increases; in general, however, awareness of a target pattern is accompanied by increases of 40 to 80 percent in brain responses (Figure 13).

In one set of experiments, no two subjects had identical response patterns. An analysis of the synchronous firing of distant neurons in small intervals of time showed extensive evidence of reentrant interactions. Although each subject had a similar response to *report* (a "representation" of either blue horizontal or red vertical bars), the patterns recorded for each subject were individual and different from those of any other subject. Although this experiment has yet to be repeated for each individual over long periods of time, it is clear that, among different individuals, each "representation," however similarly reported, was correlated with widely variant reentrant patterns.

The position and experiments I have just discussed have several consequences. The first is that, while of immense importance, neurophysiological recording cannot

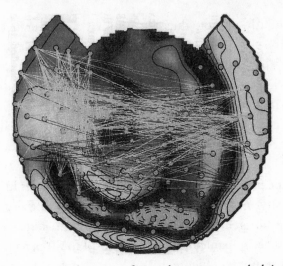

Figure 13. Coherence of neural processes underlying consciousness, measured using magnetoencephalography during binocular rivalry. The thin straight lines in white going from front to back and side to side indicate the increased synchronization that appears between distant and distributed cortical regions when the subject is conscious of a stimulus. The results are obtained by subtracting measurements when the subject was unconscious of the stimulus from the measurements made when the subject is conscious of that stimulus. The top of the plot represents the anterior regions of the cerebral cortex. The underlying dark and light regions and the contour lines reflect the intensity of the brain responses measured by the magnetic fields. These findings support the prediction made in the extended TNGS that reentry is a central mechanism underlying the conscious state.

alone capture the richness of conscious representation. This must not be misunderstood—neurophysiological analyses of covariant and causal relations in C′ are fundamental. But given the complexity and degeneracy of the environmental and bodily input to the dynamic core, there will be found no *singular* mapping for each representational state, just as there is none for similar qualia. While there are classes of neural states for a scene, it is hardly valuable to refer to such highly variable and context-dependent dynamic mappings in C′ by the term "representations."

Another consequence of this view is that much of cognitive psychology is ill-founded. There are no functional states that can be uniquely equated with defined or coded computational states in individual brains and no processes that can be equated with the execution of algorithms. Instead, there is an enormously rich set of selectional repertoires of neuronal groups whose degenerate responses can, by selection, accommodate the open-ended richness of environmental input, individual history, and individual variation. Intentionality and will, in this view, both depend on local contexts in the environment, the body, and the brain, but they can selectively arise only through such interactions, and not as precisely defined computations. Whether the self-directed movements of a fetus give rise to a "representation" of the difference between its own efforts and imposed external motions, or at the other extreme, whether particular Shakespearean metaphors and neologisms strike adults as immediately meaningful, the view that a nonrepresentational process can give rise in many ways to conscious representations is in accord with a wide range of observations and possibilities, as well as with the view that higher-order consciousness itself reached a pinnacle with the acquisition of language.

Chapter 10

Theory and the Properties of Consciousness

*I*s it possible to summarize a theory of consciousness in a short compass? I think it unlikely except if the summary is addressed to those who have already taken the long excursion. With that audience in mind, I shall try.

My first assumption has been that a biological theory of consciousness must rest on a global brain theory. This is the case because one must confront the enormous variability and individuality of higher brains and their dependence on value systems. The variability must be accounted for in terms of the principles of development and evolution. My second assumption is based on the recognition that principles of physics must be strictly obeyed and that the world defined by physics is causally closed. No spooky forces that contravene thermodynamics can be included. My argument, which does not contradict physics, has been that computer or machine models of the brain and mind do not work. Once we abandon logic and a clock, however, both of which are necessary for the operation of digital computers, we must provide an organizing principle for spatiotemporal ordering and continuity in the brain. That principle is incorporated in the process of reentry.

All of these notions are subsumed within a selectional theory of brain function, the TNGS. In this theory, the variance and individuality of brains are not noise. Instead, they are necessary contributors to neuronal repertoires made up of variant neuronal groups. Spatiotemporal coordination and synchrony are provided by reentrant interactions among these repertoires, the composition of which is determined by developmental and experiential selection. Because of the degeneracy of the neural circuits that arise dynamically as a result of these selective processes, associative interactions are guaranteed.

A theory of consciousness requires organizing principles for perceptual categorization and for value-category memory. According to the TNGS, perceptual categorization takes place by means of global mappings that connect various modal maps through reentry and also link them by non-reentrant connections to systems of motor control. According to the theory, memory is nonrepresentational, and it is necessarily associative as a result of the interactions of degenerate networks.

With these premises of the TNGS in hand, an extended theory can be formulated to deal with the neural origins of consciousness. Primary consciousness arises as a result of reentrant interactions between brain areas mediating value-category memory and those mediating perceptual categorization. A consequence of such interactions is the construction of a scene. The main source for these transactions is the dynamic core, which is based largely in the thalamocortical system. The complexity of this core is enormous, but, as a result of dynamic reentry, certain of its metastable degenerate states can yield coherent outputs and the ability to distinguish various modal combinations in a high-dimensional qualia space. That discriminatory capability within a unitary scene is exactly what the process underlying primary consciousness is proposed to be. Qualia are the discriminations entailed by that process. The individual, subjective, and privileged properties of consciousness arise in part because bodily systems are not only the earliest but also the continually prevalent sources of perceptual categorization and memory systems throughout life.

The extended TNGS claims to answer two questions: (1) How do qualia arise in an individual? (2) What is causal about the neural and mental states occurring in an individual? The extended theory claims that underlying any conscious state C is a set of neural processes C'. Given the causally closed nature of the world, it is C' that is causal, and not C. But given that it is a property entailed by C', C is the only information on C' available to a subject (Figure 14).

It is essential to recognize that, in a strict sense, C' does not cause C—there is no temporal lag in the expression of C upon occurrences of C'. The proposed mechanism by which C' gives rise to C as a property does, however, include serial temporal changes that follow from neural dynamics. This mechanism also incorporates the properties of those dynamics that follow from the binding events among cortical maps that occur through the operation of reentry. These include filling-in (as experienced, for example, in our failure to see the blind spot), as well as a variety of gestalt phenomena. All of these characteristics are reflected in the unitary nature of each conscious scene. Nevertheless, each such unitary scene is followed in short order by yet another scene and, indeed, by a host of differentiated core states resulting from the bootstrapping in time between memory and perception.

Higher-order consciousness, which allows its possessor to be conscious of being conscious, to have a socially defined nameable self, and to have a concept of the past and the future, arises by the evolution of an additional reentrant capability. This occurs when concept-forming areas involved in primary consciousness are linked by reentrant circuits to areas mediating

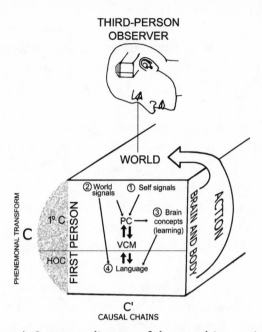

Figure 14. Summary diagram of the causal interactions of the body, brain, and environment that give rise to primary and higher-order consciousness. Causal events involve signals from the self and world leading to action on the world and interaction with other causal events (C′) in the dynamic core. The corresponding entailed properties (C) are the qualia, the high-order distinctions that constitute the phenomenal transform, represented as the dotted area on the left. Heavy arrows represent reentry; lighter arrows represent causal loops. The abbreviations used are: 1° C = primary consciousness; HOC = higher-order consciousness; PC = perceptual categorization; VCM = value-category memory.

semantic capability. Present in higher primates, it reaches its most advanced expression in humans, who possess true linguistic capability. The ability to link the tokens in a lexicon by syntactical means greatly enhances the range of reentrant expression. While the higher-order consciousness that emerges still depends on primary consciousness, having tokens and means of this kind allows an individual to become temporarily free from bondage to the remembered present.

This condensed summary is consistent with many important properties related to the conscious state. Rather than expand this account to include them, it may be more valuable to comment briefly on the testability of the extended TNGS and then to consider its explanatory power. A biological theory of consciousness must be testable across a variety of levels ranging from the molecular to the behavioral. The most efficacious tests would focus first and foremost on the demonstration of neural correlates of consciousness. As I discussed above, recent experiments at the Neurosciences Institute using magnetoencephalography to measure brain responses of human subjects when they become aware of a visual object have revealed such correlates. Perhaps the most impressive feature of the experimental results was the finding of an increase in reentrant activity across wide areas of the cortex when the subjects reported their becoming aware of an object. Experiments in other laboratories are also continually expanding our knowledge of the neural correlates of consciousness.

In addition to testability, an adequate theory must, above all, lead to understanding and provide an explanation of known properties of the conscious state. These properties fall into three feature categories, each of which I shall consider in turn. First are those properties that are shared by every conscious state, which I shall call general or fundamental properties. Second, there are properties related to the informational functions of consciousness. And, third, there are the subjective properties—those related to feelings and to notions of the self. The various properties under each category are listed in Table 1.

My aim here is to show that the extended TNGS, as summarized above, is consistent with these properties and that it provides a biological basis for each of them. I shall not explicitly deal in this account with all of the details of states such as beliefs, desires, emotions, thoughts, and so on, which are derived by interactions among these properties. Once I have shown how the various properties can be accounted for, it will not be difficult to show connections with those composite states, which philosophers call propositional attitudes.

Consider first the general properties. Each conscious state is unitary—it cannot be divided into separate parts as it is experienced. Instead, at any time, the conscious scene has unity. It is not possible, willfully or with even a high degree of attention, to limit awareness to one particular component of a scene to the exclusion of all others. Yet myriad conscious states and scenes can

Table 1. Features of conscious states

General
1. Conscious states are unitary, integrated, and constructed by the brain.
2. They can be enormously diverse and differentiated.
3. They are temporally ordered, serial, and changeable.
4. They reflect binding of diverse modalities.
5. They have constructive properties including gestalt, closure, and phenomena of filling-in.

Informational
1. They show intentionality with wide-ranging contents.
2. They have widespread access and associativity.
3. They have center-periphery, surround, and fringe aspects.
4. They are subject to attentional modulation, from focal to diffuse.

Subjective
1. They reflect subjective feelings, qualia, phenomenality, mood, pleasure, and unpleasure.
2. They are concerned with situatedness and placement in the world.
3. They give rise to feelings of familiarity or its lack.

be experienced, and conscious states follow each other in a temporal and serial order. The TNGS postulates that the reentrant dynamic core can give rise to precisely these properties as a complex system: it has parts that are functionally segregated, but within short time periods they can become increasingly integrated. Core states change from one to another within periods of hundreds of milliseconds as different circuits are activated by the environment, the body, and the brain itself. Only certain of these states are stable, and thus actually become integrated, and it is this integration that gives rise to the unitary property of C. Because the core carries out reentrant interactions between perceptual categorical input and value-category memory, both of which are continually changing, it also changes. The quasi-stable states of the core represent the binding of various modalities in different cortical regions that occurs as a result of reentrant interactions. The bound states arise from degenerate sets of circuits: contributions from all the neuronal groups within a given circuit are synchronous, but a similar output can emerge from different subsets of circuits that follow each other in a serial and asynchronous fashion. The temporal properties of consciousness arise from these processes.

These neural activities account for the unitary, integrated, yet differentiated properties of C. But it is also important to point out that, according to the TNGS, the brain necessarily must be constructive. One aspect of the integrative property of reentrant selectional networks is the appearance of filling-in and gestalt properties. Reentrant dynamics involve shifting dominances between and among cortical maps. Because of this, and because the selectional units are groups of neurons with differing properties, higher-order integrations can emerge in which one property can dominate or incorporate another. This can be seen in various visual, auditory, or somatosensory illusions. Indeed, the deliberate design of illusory inputs by neuroscientists and psychologists to emphasize certain features, as compared to the more balanced habitual input stream of signals from the environment, is likely to favor certain maps over others in a reentrant economy. Consciousness is itself an internally constructed phenomenon. By this I mean that, although perceptual input is important initially, in relatively short order the brain can go beyond the information given, or even (as in REM sleep) create conscious scenes without input from or output to the external world. Those scenes are mediated by reentrant connections to those parts of the brain that can be engaged in perception and to those involved in concept formation.

These observations point to an important problem: how can C' states that follow each other in a more or less continuous fashion give rise to the more or less smooth succession of C states without stalling or interruption? I can only put forth a conjecture: linkage of C' states involves cyclic and concatenated reentrant interactions. Such "looped" and overlapping interactions would be

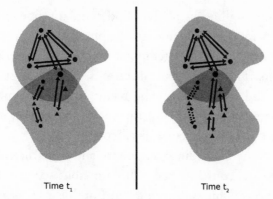

Time t_1 Time t_2

Figure 15. Hypothesis of reentrant dominance. Cyclic or concatenated reentrant paths are more likely to sustain ongoing activity than are linear paths. Dotted lines indicate a reduction or loss of reentrant signaling in linear paths not connected to cycles.

favored over linearly connected dynamic circuits, even degenerate ones (Figure 15). Although we presently lack the means to test this idea, it is worth keeping in mind.

Certain objections have been raised to the hypothesis that a unitary "continuous" or grain-free scene in the phenomenal transform might arise as a result of the discontinuous firing of discrete neurons. But a little thought about the overlapping distributions of the firings of large numbers of neuronal groups in time and space should dispel these concerns. Moreover, as a result of the dynamics of reentry, the competitive dominance of certain neuronal groups, and the contributions of categorical memory, the brain generally tends to be constructive. Filling in of the blind spot, the phenomena of apparent motion, and gestalt phenomena can all be explained in terms of temporal synchrony in reentrant circuits. The same is true of the sense of time, of succession, and of duration. The reentrant brain combines concepts and percepts with memory and new input to make a coherent picture at all costs.

Notwithstanding the unitary and constructive nature of the conscious state, the conscious scene still has enormous richness of detail. Most of this is attributable to the actual richness of signals from the physical surround as they are filtered through each sensory modality and modulated by memory. The actual content of a conscious scene obviously depends on the presence or absence of such a filter. A congenitally blind person lacking visual cortical area V4 will never know what the color red is. Yet because of the enormously parallel coincident input from the surround through hearing, touch, and motion, a blind person can construct a "space" that can serve usefully to signify a number of functions and behaviors. In general, the content of consciousness depends on whether certain cortical areas serving specific modalities are functioning normally. A person's phenomenal experience depends on these modalities and, as I have emphasized, the phenomenal aspect of these modalities cannot be reproduced by explanation. Even an accurate theory of consciousness cannot provide the blind person with an experience of redness.

All these factors account for the "irreducibility" of

consciousness and the subjective state. While some feel it necessary to "reduce" conscious experience by identifying it with neural action, this reduction leads to a category error. The origin of qualia as properties of neural processes having high-order discriminatory powers does not eliminate the subjective experience they represent.

With this account of the bases of the general properties of consciousness in hand, we can turn to what I have called informational properties—those that provide information reflecting input and output in C'. The first of these is intentionality, a term proposed by the psychologist Franz Brentano in the nineteenth century. It is the property by which consciousness is directed at, or is about, objects and states of affairs that are initially in the world. Not all forms of consciousness are intentional, and certain intentional states are not necessarily conscious. In any case, the term is not coextensive with "intending"—intending is intentional, but "intentionality" refers to a much wider range of referential states. The extended TNGS points out that the initial development of conscious states depends on interaction with perceptual categorization guided by value systems. Insofar as this fundamental aspect of higher brain function depends on input from the world and the brain through various modalities, it is not surprising that in both conscious perceptual and memorial states, intentionality is a central property. Clearly though, not all conscious states (mood, for example) are intentional.

Another aspect of the informational nature of states

underlying consciousness is their extraordinary associativity and wide access to sensation, perception, memory, imagery, and various combinations of all these. The extensive mapping of the reentrant dynamic core that is widespread over the cortex is consistent with this property. In imagery, for example, reentry essentially engages more or less the same sets of pathways that would be occupied in primary visual perception, along with other associative pathways. The property of associativity emerges from reentry and the degenerate interactions of the thalamocortical circuits that make up the core. Nonrepresentational memory also has degenerate properties that assure rich associations with a variety of circuits in addition to those involved in any particular recall.

Surround effects and the fringe at the edge of the conscious scene necessarily accompany the operations of the complex functional cluster of core activity; these are influenced by nonconscious activities of the circuits of the basal ganglia. Given the rapid changeability and metastability of core operations and the constructive nature of associative reentrant binding, fluctuations at the edge of the conscious scene would be expected. Take the eye and its movements, for example. The retina has a central region of high discriminatory power (the fovea), and the eye itself moves in fast jumps called saccades. In vision, although a scene appears fairly uniform up to the "fringe," central foveal discrimination is certainly more precise even though an individual is not aware of it. Saccades and smooth eye movements "paint" a more uniform, constructed scene as a result of the various trade-offs of brain states between precision and inclusiveness that occur after the brain receives signals from the optic nerve. This is another example of constructive filling-in, which must have variation at its edges.

This brings us to the complex issue of attention, which I believe has multiple mechanisms. These range from the relatively diffuse C states that result from the C' states mediated by corticocortical interactions, to those gated via the reticular nucleus of the thalamus, to the most highly focal states of the core influenced by the motor cortical circuitry of the basal ganglia. We are not aware of those "blocked" motor states, but the theory suggests that it is the engagement of the core with circuits lacking output to muscles that forms the basis of the most focal of attentive conscious states. In these focal states, the core is modulated to such a degree that the experience is as if one is anesthetized deeply to all aspects of an image, scene, or thought but the one that is focally attended. The exact mechanism by which such modulation occurs is not known. One possibility is that the inhibitory output of global mappings to the thalamus via the basal ganglia allows certain core responses to occur at the expense of others. The details remain to be worked out. In any event, it is likely that attention is effected through a variety of different routes and mechanisms. I have already discussed the interactive aspects of attentive learning and automaticity, which are connected to the question of how automatic routines previously learned by conscious attentive means are recalled and linked together consciously. The notion that this is achieved by interactions between the thalamocortical core and the basal ganglia (which may also engage the cerebellum) is one that still requires testing.

I turn now to properties related to subjectivity. The phenomenal transform of C' to C through the earliest categorical experiences of bodily perceptions is one of the major origins of the subjective sense and the notion of the self. I have made the statement that all conscious experience partakes of multiple qualia and that a single quale, say "red," cannot be the sole aspect of conscious experience. According to the extended TNGS, we experience a multidimensional qualia space and consciousness reflects our ability to make high-order discriminations, which are the qualia within that space. Obviously, different sensory modalities lead to different discriminatory capabilities. Their content depends particularly upon the range of cortical interactions of the dynamic core, which is modulated by attention. This is consistent both with the unitary property of the conscious scene and its differentiability.

The question arises as to the continued central role of the self through contributions of the body, the environment, and memory. There are two contributions that appear to be fundamental. One is the phenomenal transform acted upon by various modalities and, early on, by value systems, autonomic responses, and proprioception (see Figures 7 and 10). These systems, concerned as they are with bodily regulation, must continue to operate throughout life in parallel with other inputs from sensory modalities.

The phenomenal contribution to self-reference is enhanced by a second contribution—the Piagetian notion of self—the distinction made between internally generated directed movement and motions induced from outside sources. This discrimination may actually originate in utero during the late fetal stages, but certainly occurs during early postnatal development. It provides a reference for distinguishing self from nonself through kinesthetic inputs that may act in addition to, and separately from, explicit sensory contributions to qualia space.

A third form of self-discrimination is likely to emerge later in development as a property of higher-order consciousness. This is the conscious process of individuation—the recognition of other selves and other minds. The TNGS has no difficulty in accounting for this last process in terms of the connection between emotions, learning, and social influences on development of the self, at least in semantically equipped species.

Well before such social developments, the origin of a sense of situatedness and of familiarity can be linked to both the phenomenal and the voluntary motor aspects of self-development. Of course, much remains to be learned about the detailed mechanisms underlying the perceptual categorization of states of the body. It is already clear that memory systems, interacting with internal input from the various regulatory systems of the body, can render such categorizations omnipresent. Moreover, emotional responses interacting with value systems and the homeostatic functions of the brain play key roles in both primary and higher-order consciousness.

Finally, in considering the entries in Table 1, a few additional points are worth stressing. While the fundamental and general properties of consciousness cannot be relinquished, there are shifting degrees of contribution from each of the informational and subjective properties. These shifts are related to alterations in value systems, learning experiences, emotions, and fluctuations in attentional mechanisms. Obviously, the variations across conscious properties with experience can be very great depending on inputs to the dynamic core.

It is not difficult to imagine how, from such mixtures and varying interactions among the properties in Table 1, one can discern the origins of complex mental states such as beliefs, desires, and emotional responses. Given experience and the existence of linguistic skills, it is perhaps not too far-fetched to imagine how even logical thought might have emerged from their interactions during experience. It remains to be seen how closely such connections can be established. The obvious point is that consciousness and its underlying C′ states are central to all of these complex expressions, both rational and irrational.

Chapter 11

Identity

THE SELF, MORTALITY, AND VALUE

*I*n addition to providing an analysis of causation and the phenomenal transform, a theory of consciousness must account for subjectivity. This is not simple identity or individuality. It is the possession of a unique conscious history whose underlying neural states are capable of refined discriminations that affect behavior at the same time as they give rise to subjective feelings.

Given the nature of inheritance and evolutionary selection, every multicellular organism may be said to have a unique biological identity. In animals with an adaptive immune system, that identity is essential for survival. But until cognitive systems arose in evolution and consciousness appeared, the activity of a freely behaving self with richly idiosyncratic behavior, while impressive, was nonetheless limited. It is true that learning and communication systems arose in evolution well before primary consciousness. Organisms such as bees or wasps can, for example, show remarkable adaptive behavior in groups that depends to some degree on individual variation. But the outcome in groups such as eusocial insects is less autonomous and more statistical in nature than the behavior of individual conscious animals.

We do not know at what point in evolutionary history primary consciousness first arose. However, by comparing homologous neural structures required for its expression in humans and other vertebrates (for example, a thalamocortical system and ascending value systems along with certain behavioral patterns), we can put forth a tenable conjecture that primary consciousness appeared in vertebrates first at the transition between reptiles and birds, and second at the transition between reptiles and mammals.

The ability to construct a scene related to the value-category history of an individual marks the appearance of the self. An organism with a self can make rich discriminations based on its past learning history and can use consciousness to plan, at least in the period represented by the remembered present. The complex integration of the dynamic core, modulated by behavioral history and the memories of individual learning events, leads to adaptive behavior that is necessarily idiosyncratic for that individual organism.

The basis for individual emotional responses rests with the diffuse ascending-value systems, such as the locus coeruleus, the raphé nuclei, the various cholinergic and dopaminergic systems, and several hypothalamic systems. Other autonomic systems and brainstem nuclei controlling bodily responses also provide a key basis for the homeostatic, cardiorespiratory, and hormonal activities that modulate emotion. In addition to the signals provided by these essential self-regulating systems of the brain, there are also the proprioceptive and kinesthetic responses accompanying various movements. An individual with dawning primary consciousness already receives "self-inputs" from such systems of motor control. As I already mentioned, it may even be that a spontaneously moving fetus in late development distinguishes between brain inputs arising from self-generated bodily movements and those inputs generated by motions induced from without. There is enough evidence to make the case that input from value systems and proprioceptive systems can combine with modal sensory inputs to yield some of the earliest conscious experiences. It is likely that such fundamental adaptive systems remain central for the rest of an individual's conscious life, whatever the additional qualia may be that develop with ongoing experience.

If this is the case, the individual self necessarily has a "point of view" that, given the activity of the dynamic core, is integrated and generally persistent. Thus, if one asks whether the appearance of a scene in primary consciousness has a "witness," the answer is likely to be that the witness is constituted in an ongoing fashion by the integrated bodily responses considered above as they relate to those from memory and perceptual input. Indeed, it must be said that the idea of a "witness" is, to some degree, anomalous: the first person is simply present. Given the continual sensorimotor signals arising from the body, subjectivity is a baseline event that is never extinguished in the normal life of conscious individuals. But there is no need for an inner observer or "central I"—in James's words, "the thoughts themselves are the thinker."

Of course, in animals without semantic abilities, higher-order consciousness cannot be present. A self derived from primary consciousness is not able to symbolize its memory states, or become truly self-conscious or conscious of being conscious. When the necessary reentrant circuits evolved in higher primates and finally in Homo sapiens, a *concept* of the self appeared along with concepts of the past and future. Although as conscious humans, we experience the Heraclitean illusion consisting of a point in present time advancing from the past into the future, a little reflection will show that an actual coupling to physical space-time can only occur in the "remembered present" of primary consciousness. For an animal with higher-order consciousness the past and future are conceptual constructs.

One must avoid the temptation of splitting and

over-defining mental states and representations. Higher-order consciousness that is reflected by qualia in a high-dimensional space, and which is integrated to yield a scene having a focal center with shifting fringes and on-going changes, can never be focused to just one precise token. You cannot, for example, be aware of just a red spot and nothing else. The constructive integration that leads to a unitary representation incorporating many distinctions has more adaptive significance to the individual than any such limited designator or token, however precise.

Thus, there is adaptive value in such multidimensional and situated discriminations. What they lack in absolute precision, they make up for by enhancing our ability to generalize, to imagine, and to communicate in a rich environment. Higher-order consciousness may be considered as a trade-off of absolute precision for rich imaginative possibilities. Although our unitary conscious scene is not necessarily veridical, for purposes of planning and creative scenario building it gains added power even as it gives up precision. I do not believe that this is an incidental point. The pervasive presence of degeneracy in biological systems is particularly notice-able in neural systems, and it exists to a high degree in the reentrant selective circuits of the conscious brain. In certain circumstances, natural languages gain as much strength from ambiguity as they do under other circumstances through the power of logical definition. Association and metaphor are powerful accompaniments of conscious experience even at very early stages, and they flower with linguistic experience.

What is particularly striking about the operations of the conscious human brain is the necessity for integration, for a unitary picture, for construction, and for closure. This is manifested by the obliviousness we have to our blind spot, by various visual, somatosensory, and auditory illusions, and most strikingly, by neuropsychological syndromes. The patient with anosognosia and hemineglect who denies ownership of a paralyzed left hand and arm, the patient with somatoparaphrenia who insists that a touch on an anesthetic and paralyzed left hand is a touch on her sister's hand not on hers, or the patient with alien hand syndrome—none of these individuals is psychotic even if, in certain respects, each fails the test of veridicality. The conscious brain in health and disease will integrate what can be integrated and resists a fractured or shattered view of "reality." I believe that these phenomena are reflections of the necessity for global reentrant circuits to form closed cycles with whatever brain areas and maps are left to be integrated. Illusions can be induced in normal persons by manipulation of world and body signals. As I have already discussed, I believe that illusions reflect the shifts in patterns of dominance among interactive reentrant maps. The take-home lesson is that our body, our brain, and our consciousness did not evolve to yield a scientific picture of the world. Instead, sufficient adaptation to an econiche is what saves the day, even in the presence of emotions and imaginings that would be irrelevant or unavailable to a precise third-person description.

In animals with higher-order consciousness such as ourselves, these operations provide a rich mixture of images, feelings, memories, pleasure and displeasure, beliefs, and intentions—all of the intentional states as well as those of moods. No two socially defined selves (necessarily socially defined in a speech community) will ever have identical brain states—the C′ states that entail C states. But such individuals can exchange information even on the basis of the mistaken belief that their C states are causal. This belief is safe, even if scientifically false, for evolution has set up reentrant circuits to yield C states as properties of C′ states. Indeed, C states are the only reliable informational means we have of accessing our C′ states.

This view is not paradoxical, nor does it qualify as dualism or as the weirdly detached epiphenomenology that so distresses physicalist philosophers. C states are necessarily entailed by C′ states, and the self has access to the causal consequences of C′ states through C states. It will be a long time, if ever, before neurophysiology using on-line recording is so advanced that we can predict the next C′ state (or C state, for that matter) in anywhere near a determinative fashion. Nonetheless, with further experimentation, larger patterns in C′ states that are neural correlates of consciousness will continue to be uncovered.

If this brain-based picture of how the self arises

turns out to be correct, there is, of course, one dreary consequence: We are mortal. Once the substrate for C states is dissolved, the self, which is a dynamic process, ceases to be. There are some who find this conclusion distasteful to the same degree as others find it repellant to accept the idea that we are not computers. Higher-order consciousness certainly allows for beliefs that are contrary-to-fact. Let each self find its consolation in its own way. Whatever belief system we espouse, the richness of individual experiences during our lifetime continues to be precious and irreplaceable.

There is a final point, which is not separate from the need for immortality or its dismissal. This concerns the place of value in a world of facts. Scientific world pictures based on the generality of physics alone have no need for value, nor do they show evidence for it in the inanimate universe. If our picture of conscious organisms and of evolution is correct, however, value systems are necessary constraints, both for evolutionary selection and for neuronal group selection in animals with higher brains. This does not mean, however, that higher-order social values are genetically specified. Instead, it means that such values will arise under the constraints of adaptive systems, particularly those of conscious individuals. While there is a biological basis for values, it is only through historical encounter and social exchange as humans that we can build on such values to yield rights. On at least one planet in the universe, the evolutionary emergence of the reentrant dynamic core with its C′ states has assured the place of value in a world of facts. Indeed, from a causal point of view, the reverse is also true—only as a result of value systems in a selectional brain can the bases emerge for the phenomenal gift of consciousness.

Chapter 12

Mind and Body

SOME CONSEQUENCES

Many confusions about the mind-body problem are linguistic in origin. Others have to do with misunderstanding of the procedures we must adapt in studying consciousness. Unlike physics, which assumes consciousness and perception and takes a God's-eye view of its domain, the study of consciousness must recognize the first-person, or subjective, point of view. As a third-person observer studying another person's consciousness (see Figure 14), I must *assume* that that person has mental processes similar to my own. I must then construct a variety of experimental procedures to test the reports made by the subject, searching for consistencies in his or her neural or psychological responses.

A theory of consciousness based on these efforts must not conflict with the known laws of physics, chemistry, or biology. Specifically, it must accept the fact that the physical world is causally closed—only forces and energies can be causally effective. Consciousness is a property of neural processes and cannot itself act causally in the world. As a process and an entailed property, consciousness arose during the evolution of complex neural networks with a specific kind of structure and dynamics. Before consciousness could emerge, certain neural arrangements must have evolved. These arrangements lead to reentrant interactions, and it is the dynamics of reentrant networks that provide the causal bases that entail conscious properties. Such networks were chosen during evolution because they provided animals with the ability to make high-level discriminations, an ability that afforded adaptive advantages in dealing with novelty and planning.

Consciousness reflects the ability to make distinctions or discriminations among huge sets of alternatives. These distinctions are made in fractions of a second and they vary continually. As a series of phenomenal experiences, consciousness is necessarily private—it is tied to an individual's body and brain and to the history of that individual's environmental interactions. That history is unique—two different individuals of a species, even twins, cannot identically share the same conscious state. Indeed, the likelihood of any two conscious states being identical, even in one individual, is infinitesimally small. In this view, while no mental change can occur without an underlying neural change, the converse is not necessarily the case. Many neural changes have no effect on the phenomenal character of the conscious state as reflected in qualia.

Qualia are high-order distinctions, and the scenes of consciousness can be looked upon as a series of qualia. Such a series is experienced over a vast number of events signaling from the world, the body, and the brain itself. The multiplicity and potential parallelism of these events are both of high order, and the qualia that are included in an integrated but varying scene cover a wide range of experiences. They include perceptions, images, memories, sensations, emotions, moods, thoughts, beliefs, desires, intentions, motor scenarios, and rich signals—however vague—of bodily states. These varied experiences may at first seem too disparate to be encompassed by the mechanisms for the emergence of consciousness that are proposed here. But it must be remembered that, in a highly connected complex system like the brain, integration of the combinatorial interactions of cortical and subcortical areas can result in an enormous number of states.

The function of the reentrant dynamic core, whether in primary or higher-order consciousness, can be modulated by the brain mechanisms underlying focal attention and memory. Subcortical structures such as the thalamus and basal ganglia can mediate attentional narrowing of core states. In this sense, conscious states depend as heavily on nonconscious mechanisms of attention as they do on the nonconscious mechanisms of perceptual categorization.

Inasmuch as consciousness arises as a result of reentry in the dynamic core, it is necessarily integrated by reentry. To the subject, consciousness appears as a unitary process and, because of the binding and synchrony that result from reentry, the brain is constructive.

However, as I have mentioned, certain syndromes showing aberrant conscious states can emerge from alterations of the core and its interactions with nonconscious substrates. In such pathological states, or even in induced states such as those of a hypnotic trance, the core can split into a small number of separate cores, or even be remodeled constructively. Splitting of the core definitely occurs in disconnection syndromes that result from cutting the corpus callosum and anterior commissure. It is also likely to be a main basis of dissociative syndromes such as hysteria. Core remodeling can occur in neuropsychological syndromes such as blindsight, prosopagnosia, hemineglect, and anosognosia. In such syndromes, it is likely that the dominant reentrant reactions of the core are redistributed constructively, resulting in a reallocation of conscious and nonconscious capacities.

In both normal and abnormal states, the brain of

an experienced individual attends continually to signals from the body and the environment, but even more to signals from itself. Whether in the dreams of REM sleep, or in imagery, or even in perceptual categorization, a variety of sensory, motor, and higher-order conceptual processes are constantly in play. Given the mechanisms underlying memory and consciousness, both sensory and motor elements are always engaged. For example, in perception, there are contributions of motor elements—not acted out—that result from the premotor contributions of global mappings. And in visual imagery, the same reentrant circuits used in direct perception are reengaged, but without the more precise constraints of signals from without. In REM sleep, the brain truly speaks to itself in a special conscious state—one constrained neither by outside sensory input nor by the tasks of motor output.

In all of these processes, primary consciousness is continually related to temporal change. It has a diachronic structure and is necessarily historical. Primary consciousness is, however, tied only to successive intervals of present time—the remembered present. The lag of up to five hundred milliseconds that is found between intended action, neural response, and conscious awareness is not a paradox if one understands the relationship between nonconscious automaticity and conscious planning. Consciousness is not involved in automatic motor processes (except during the learning leading to automaticity), but instead is related to planning and to the creation of new combinations of already automatic routines.

I have stated in the Preface of this small book that my hope is to disenthrall those who believe that the subject of consciousness is exclusively metaphysical or necessarily mysterious. It is a Herculean task for consciousness studies to rid the stables of dualism, mysterianism, paranormal projections, and unnecessary appeals to as yet poorly characterized properties at different material scales—for example, quantum gravity. Some but not all of this task relates to the use of language. In this account, for example, I must answer to the accusation that I have submitted to the paradoxes of epiphenomenalism. This notion, a cousin of dualism and a prompting ground for "zombie-speak," must be reexamined. I believe that the difficulties with this notion have arisen because of the failure to attend to the neural correlates of conscious properties. Inasmuch as the neural process C' that entails consciousness C is causal and reliable, we do not find ourselves faced with a paradox. C' underlies the ability to make distinctions in a complex domain, and C states, the properties entailed by C', *are* those distinctions.

This relationship allows us to talk of C *as if* it is causal. For most situations, this is not dangerous, given the reliability of the relationship. Only when we are tempted to abrogate physics or give to C mystical powers is this procedure hazardous. The relation of entailment between C' and C clarifies the issue and helps define qualia as higher-order discriminations with distinct and specific neural bases. A consciousness-free zombie, on these grounds, is logically impossible—if it had C′ processes they would necessarily entail C. Of course, I am aware of the fact that the clarification introduced by this analysis must be proven by actual experiments on the relation between C′ and C. But like the proportionality constant of mass in the equation $F = mA$ and the assumption of the constancy of the velocity of light in a vacuum, the foregoing analysis promises a simplification and coordination of one of the most challenging problems of science.

Needless to say, I am aware of those who expect such a scientific analysis to explain the "actual feeling of a quale"—the warmness of warmth and the greenness of green. My reply remains the same: these are the properties of the phenotype, and any phenotype that is conscious experiences its own differential qualia because those qualia *are* the distinctions made. It suffices to explain the bases of these distinctions—just as it suffices in physics to give an account of matter and energy, not why there is something rather than nothing. This our theory can do by pointing out the differences in neural structures and dynamics underlying different modalities and brain functions.

Finally, some general remarks may be in order. The view I have taken emphasizes the constructive, irreversible, variable, yet creative properties of the brain. These are properties that can be explained on the basis of a selectional theory of brain function such as neural Darwinism. This theory argues against any simple-minded reduction of historical events inasmuch as it is based on population thinking and Darwinian evolution. Moreover, it is worth pointing out that the occurrence of C as an entailed property of C′ does not contravene esthetic or ethical judgments inasmuch as the constraints of conscious systems such as C′ depend ultimately on value systems.

In line with these reflections, I have previously suggested that there are two main modes of thought—logic and selectionism (or pattern recognition). Both are powerful, but it is pattern recognition that can lead to creation, for example, in the choice of axioms in mathematics. While logic can prove theorems when embedded in computers, it cannot choose axioms. Even if it cannot create axioms, it is useful in taming the excesses of creative pattern making. Because the brain can function by pattern recognition even prior to language, brain activity can yield what might be called "pre-metaphorical" capabilities. The power of such analogical abilities, particularly when ultimately translated into language, rests in the associativity that results from the degeneracy of neural networks. The products of the ensuing metaphorical abilities, while necessarily ambiguous, can be richly creative. As I have stressed, logic can be used to tame the excesses of those products, but cannot itself be creative to the same degree. If selectionism is the mistress of our thoughts, logic is their housekeeper. A balance between these two modes of thought and the endless riches of their underlying neural substrates can be sampled through conscious experience. Even if, someday, we are able to embed both these modes in the construction of a conscious artifact and thus further extend our comprehension, the particular forms of consciousness that we possess as humans will not be reproducible and will continue to be our greatest gift.

Glossary

Action potential. An electrical impulse traveling down a neuron's membrane conducting signals from cell bodies to synapses.

Adaptive immune system. The means by which vertebrates recognize foreign molecules, viruses, and bacteria and react to them. Immune systems achieve this by constructing a large repertoire of antibodies, each with a particular potential binding site.

Anosognosia. A syndrome characterized by denial by a patient of illness or unawareness of its existence. Seen particularly in some patients with strokes affecting the right cortical hemisphere.

Aphasia. Impairment or loss of the capacity to produce or understand language following brain damage.

Areas: prefrontal, parietal, temporal, visual, auditory, somatosensory, motor. Regions of the cerebral cortex mediating one or more aspects of sensory or motor responses.

Areas are designated primary if they are the first to receive projections from the thalamus.

Association areas. Regions of cortex that do not include primary sensory or motor areas.

Associativity. The property of connecting or correlating various brain regions, functions, or memories.

Attention. The ability to consciously select certain features from the vast array of sensory signals presented to the brain.

Automaticity. The conversion of behavior after conscious rehearsal to nonconscious behavioral routines. Reflected in some aspects of **procedural memory.**

Autonomic nervous system. The visceral, mainly involuntary, system of nerves consisting of sympathetic and parasympathetic divisions controlling the internal environment. The first is for "fight or flight" reactions, the second is for "rest and digest." Regulated mainly by the **hypothalamus.**

Axon. Structurally an extended neuronal process that carries action potentials to a synapse.

Basal ganglia. A linked collection of five large nuclei at the center of the forebrain that serve to regulate motor acts and automatic responses that are nonconscious by interacting through the thalamus with the cortex.

Binding problem. How can different cortical areas and modalities act synchronously and coherently (simultaneously for movement, color, orientation, and so on) despite the fact that each is specified by separate regions and there is no superordinate or executive area? Plausibly solved by **reentry.**

Binocular rivalry. The alternation over time of the perception of two disparate inputs (for example, vertical bars versus horizontal bars) presented simultaneously to different eyes.

Bipedal posture. The upright stance in which the hind limbs bear weight and carry out walking, freeing the upper limbs from these functions.

Blindsight. In certain patients, conscious visual experience is entirely lost for all or part of the visual field, yet the ability to respond more or less accurately to visual stimuli under test conditions remains.

Brain dynamics. The functional (that is, electrical and chemical) complex of activities as distinguished from the anatomy within which these activities are carried out.

Brain scans. Various techniques for noninvasively following brain dynamics in living subjects. These techniques include functional magnetic resonance imaging (fMRI) and magnetoencephalography (MEG).

Brainstem. A part of the brain made up of the thalamus, the hypothalamus, the midbrain, and the hindbrain. The hindbrain includes the cerebellum, pons, and medulla, but the cerebellum is generally excluded from the definition.

Broca's area. An area in the left frontal lobe, damage to which leads to difficulties in speech production or motor aphasia.

C and C′. C designates any conscious process; C′ designates its underlying neural activity.

Causal efficacy. The action in the physical world of forces or energies that lead to effects or physical outcomes.

Causality. According to the laws of physics, the causal order is closed—that is, it cannot be affected directly by mental properties such as **qualia.**

Cell body. The part of a neuron containing the nucleus with its DNA.

Cell migration. The patterned movement of neurons or their cellular precursors during the formation of the brain.

Cerebellum. A large structure attached to the brainstem that contributes to the coordination of motor activity.

Cerebral cortex. A six-layered mantle of neurons (gray matter) over the surface of the cerebral hemispheres. The mantle is folded into convoluted protrusions (gyri) and clefts (sulci).

Channel. A molecular structure (a protein) in the cell membrane that allows ions to pass from one side to the other.

Cholinergic nuclei. Collections of neurons activated by the neurotransmitter acetylcholine.

Clone. The asexual progeny of a single cell.

Closure; filling-in. The tendency of the brain to integrate signals with whatever interactions are available to it. Filling-in is found in the failure to notice the blind spot; other examples include cases of denial such as those found in **anosognosia.**

Coarticulated sounds. Sounds that simultaneously have complex mixtures of different frequencies and energies, such as human speech or vocal sounds.

Coherence. The simultaneous or synchronous activity of distant collections of neurons or other agents.

Combinatorial. Mathematical operations quantitatively describing the various interactions of different systems or parts.

Complexity. A property of any system composed of multiple heterogeneous smaller parts that nonetheless interact to give integrated outcomes.

Computations. In a narrow sense, the actions carried out by a digital computer processing algorithms via a program.

Computer. A device (here, a digital computer that consists of hardware and software) utilizing collections of algorithms or effective procedures making up a program that performs logical operations to yield an output. See also **Turing machine.**

Concatenated reentrant loops. Reentrant structures that form cycles that overlap with one another.

Concept. Usually refers to propositions expressing abstract or general ideas. Used here to refer to the brain's ability to categorize its own perceptual activities and construct a "universal."

Corpus callosum. A large fiber system connecting similar areas of the right and left cerebral hemispheres. Cutting or destroying this bundle leads to the disconnection syndromes shown by split-brain patients.

Correlation. A statistical term used to describe and quantify nonrandom relations between two systems.

Cortex: primary, secondary, tertiary. Somewhat old-fashioned terms distinguishing the portions or areas of the cortex receiving direct sensory input or mediating direct output (primary cortex) from "higher" areas that connect to these areas (association cortex).

Cortical hemispheres. The two (left and right) large structures, making up a good portion of the forebrain, which have the cerebral cortex as their mantle.

Corticostriatal. Axonal projection from the cortex to the input nuclei of the basal ganglia (the so-called striatum).

Covariance. A statistical term quantifying the mutual change in two or more variables.

Degeneracy. The ability of different structures to carry out the same function or yield the same output.

Dendrite. One of the many postsynaptic (input) branches of a neuron that receives axonal connections to form a synapse at sites called dendritic spines.

Developmental selection. The first tenet of the **TNGS.** It refers to the creation of large repertoires of variant circuits in the microanatomy of the brain during development.

Differentiable; differentiated. Used to refer to the fact that conscious experience can change from one unitary scene to another in an apparently limitless fashion. See **Unitary.**

Direct and indirect pathways. Two main routes of connections within the basal ganglia leading to stimulation or inhibition of thalamic nuclei by basal ganglion activity.

Discrimination. The capacity of conscious systems to categorize, distinguish, or differentiate among a multitude of signals or patterns in terms of integrated scenes and qualia.

Distributed system. Widespread and separated neuronal groups that can nonetheless interact through connections to give an integrated response or output (see **Complexity**). The cortex is a distributed system.

Dopaminergic nuclei. Four major systems of brain neurons utilizing the neurotransmitter dopamine. They constitute a value system involved in the reward systems of learning. Dopaminergic synapses are considered targets of antipsychotic drugs, particularly for schizophrenia.

Dualism. The belief that the facts of the world cannot be explained except through the existence of two different and irreducible principles. In philosophy, its most noted exponent was René Descartes, who divided the world into *res extensa* (subject to physics) and *res cogitans* (not so accessible).

Dynamic core. A term used in the extended TNGS to refer to a system of interactions, figured mainly in the thalamocortical system, which behaves as a **functional cluster.** The core sends signals mainly to itself, and its reentrant interactions are assumed to give rise to conscious states.

Econiche. The part of the environment in which a species acts and within which natural selection occurs.

Embodiment. The view that the mind, brain, body, and environment all interact to yield behavior. Used in some sense to contradict the idea of a "disembodied mind" or dualistic consciousness.

Emotion. The complex of feeling, cognition, and bodily responses reflecting the action of value systems within the conscious brain. The term comprises a huge range of responses, of which the examples are obvious and known to the reader.

Enkephalin. A small peptide, member of a set of endogenous opioids (opiate-like substances produced by the brain). Their actions can produce analgesia or blunting of pain.

Entailment. A relationship of implication used here in regard to the relationship between C' processes and **C.** C' entails C as a property. Thus, C (consciousness) is entailed by physical processes in the brain, mainly in the **dynamic core.**

Entropy. In physics, a measure of order or disorder. In information theory, a measure of the reduction of uncertainty. Entropy can be related to the number of different states of a system weighted by their probability of occurrence.

Epigenetic. Biological processes that do not depend directly upon gene expression. An example: "neurons that fire together, wire together."

Epiphenomenal. Lacking in causal effectiveness. For example, the lights flashing on a computer console could be removed without affecting its internal processing. Philosophers argue about whether C is epiphenomenal and some find this paradoxical. This book makes the case that, properly understood, there is no paradox.

Episodic memory. The memory of past events, mediated by the interaction of the hippocampus with the cerebral cortex. Removal of the hippocampus obliterates the capacity to form such memories from the time of the operation (or lesion) forward.

Evolution. The process underlying the emergence and survival of living things. Accounted for by several theories attributable to Charles Darwin, of which the central one is **natural selection.**

Experiential selection. The second tenet of the **TNGS,** which states that a secondary repertoire of functioning neural circuits is formed on the basis of existing neuroanatomy by means of the selective strengthening and weakening of synaptic efficacies.

Explanatory gap. A term used by philosophers to stress the difficulty or impossibility of relating conscious phenomena to the neural workings of the brain.

Feedback. A term used strictly in control theory to designate correction of a deviation in output by an error signal derived from a sample of that output. For example, if an amplifier is to amplify a sine wave and the output is distorted, an error signal is sent back through a single channel to modify the dynamics to yield the correct waveform. Feedback always operates from an output to an earlier stage, whereas **reentry** may occur between stages operating in parallel at the same or different levels in a system. In popular use, the term feedback is applied indiscriminately and often vaguely to any correction of input by a reverse signal.

First-person experience. The privacy of an individual's stream of consciousness, which cannot be shared directly by a third-person observer.

fMRI (functional magnetic resonance imaging). A noninvasive scanning method for observing brain dynamics by using magnetic resonance imaging to record changes in blood oxygen levels that are correlated with neural activity.

Focal attention. An attentional state directed strongly toward a single object, thought, or experience.

Fourier transform. A mathematical operation for dealing

analytically with functions (waves, for example) by converting them to sums of sine and cosine functions.

Frequency tag. A method used in MEG and EEG (electroencephalography) to mark a brain response as one reflecting a given signal. In MEG, for example, oscillating a signal at 7 Hz (seven times a second) will show a sharp spike at that frequency in an ensuing record of brain activity analyzed by Fourier transforms.

Freudian unconscious. A domain of which a subject is not conscious but that is capable of being made conscious by psychoanalytic techniques.

Fringe. Used by William James to denote the "influence of a faint brain process on our thoughts," as it makes us "aware of relations and objects but dimly perceived."

Functional cluster. In complexity theory, a system or part of a system that interacts mainly with itself. The **dynamic core** is a functional cluster.

Functional connectivity. Paths within a neuroanatomical network that actually reflect neural dynamics, for example, input yielding output.

Functional segregation. Relative restriction of the activity of a brain area to a given function. For instance, one visual area may be functionally segregated for colors, another for object movement, and so on.

GABA. Gamma-aminobutyric acid. An inhibitory neurotransmitter found, for example, in the local inhibitory circuits of the cortex and those of the basal ganglia.

Genetic code. The set of rules by which DNA sequences specify amino-acid sequences in proteins. The code consists of non-overlapping triplets (for example, AUG for methionine and UUU for phenylalanine). There are sixty-four triplets, or codons, and twenty amino acids, and the code is therefore degenerate (see **Degeneracy**).

Gestalt phenomena. Aspects of perception in which simple sensory inputs can be grouped in particular ways to create a gestalt, a figure or form that is not a property of the observed object but reflects the constructive capabilities of the brain.

Gestural communication. Exchanging messages through gestures, as in mime or, when syntactically organized, sign language.

Glia. The supporting cells of the nervous system necessary for biochemical and energetic as well as structural functions, but not for signaling by action potentials. There are several types, including astrocytes and oligodendrocytes.

Global mapping. A term referring to the smallest structures in the brain capable of **perceptual categorization.** Reflects the activity of multiple reentrant maps, motor and sensory, linked to nonreentrant structures and finally to muscles and sensory receptors capable, through movement, of sampling a world of stimuli.

Globus pallidus. A part of the basal ganglia. It receives connections from the caudate nucleus and sends projections to the ventrolateral nucleus of the thalamus.

Glutamate. The main excitatory neurotransmitter of the central nervous system.

Hebb synapse. Named after Donald Hebb, a psychologist who enunciated Hebb's rule: When an axon of cell A excites cell B and persistently takes part in firing it, a change occurs in one or both cells so that A's efficiency in firing B is increased. A Hebb synapse follows this rule.

Hemineglect. Certain patients with damage to the right parietal cortex no longer pay attention to or seem aware of the left side of a scene.

Heraclitean illusion. The notion of a point in time smoothly flowing from the past through the present to the future. This is illusory in that only the present is directly accessible to experience, whereas the past and the future are concepts.

High-dimensional space. We live in four-dimensional space-time (three of space, one of time). Qualia space is a high-dimensional or n-dimensional space, where n is the number of axes along which distinctions can be made; n is much greater than four.

Higher-order consciousness. The capability to be conscious of being conscious. This capacity is present in animals with semantic abilities (chimpanzees) or linguistic abilities (humans), and those with linguistic abilities are also able to have a social concept of the self and concepts of the past and future. Distinguished from **primary consciousness.**

Hippocampus. A sausage-shaped neural structure lying along the anteromedial region of each temporal lobe. In cross section it resembles a sea horse, hence the name. Necessary for episodic memory.

Homeostatic. Tending to maintain constancy in the status of the interior environment, whether of cells or tissues.

Hominines. A group within the order Primates that includes modern humans and their antecedents, who appeared after the divergence from precursors of the apes.

Homologous structures. Distinct structures evolutionarily derived from a common ancestor, in respect to structure or function. The thalami of dogs and mice are homologous to those of humans.

Hox **and** ***Pax*** **Genes.** Ancient genes that regulate morphogenesis. *Pax* 6, for example, is essential for normal development of the eye. *Hox* genes regulate the structures of the hindbrain. Their expression in the embryo is place dependent.

Huntington's disease. A hereditary disease involving the degeneration of the caudate and putamen of the basal ganglia. It leads to continual involuntary movements (chorea) and progressive dementia, and ends with death.

Hypothalamus. A set of nuclei below the thalamus that affect feeding, sex, sleep, emotional expression, endocrine functions, and even movement. A value system.

Ideal or perfect gas. A theoretical construct consisting of randomly colliding particles whose collisions are perfectly elastic and exchange no **mutual information.**

Identity. All animals that are not twins are genetically non-identical, and each individual is therefore unique. This can be the case without having a conscious self.

Illusion. Psychophysically manipulated signals that lead to a perception of features not physically verifiable. They are "false" expressions of "real" sensory input. The illusory contours of a Kanizsa triangle are an example, and so is a Necker cube. Illusions can occur in various modalities and range from simple to complex.

Information. In present usage, the reduction of uncertainty conveyed by a message.

Inhibitory loops. Neurons linked by inhibitory synapses and connected in loops. The classical example is provided by the basal ganglia, whose polysynaptic loops either can be inhibitory or can inhibit inhibition (disinhibition).

Instructionism. The idea that information from structures that are to be recognized is necessary in constructing a recognition system. An example is the idea, now disproven, that antibodies are specific because they wrap around the shapes of antigens when these antibodies are formed. The opposite of instructionism is selectionism as represented by the theory of evolution and the TNGS.

Integration. In complexity theory, the measure of mutual information or entropy reduction in a system. In brain science, the relating, correlation, or connection of signals to yield a unitary output.

Intensity. A measure of strength. In electromagnetic measurements, such as **magnetoencephalography,** the intensity is the square root of the **power.**

Intentionality. The idea proposed by Franz Brentano that consciousness refers to particular objects—it is about things. This is not the same as "intending."

Intralaminar nuclei. Nuclei of the thalamus that project diffusely to the frontal cortex, caudate, and putamen. Probably concerned with setting thresholds of their targets and thus implicated in the maintenance of consciousness.

Irreducibility. A theory or statement is irreducible if it cannot be fully accounted for by a theory at some lower level of organization.

Jamesian properties. Consciousness is a form of awareness, is continuous but continually changing, is private, has **intentionality,** and does not exhaust the properties of its objects.

Kinesthetic. Relating to perception of movement or position of joints, or limbs, or body.

Language. In strict use, a vehicle of communication that has phonology (or signing), semantics, and syntax. Humans are the only species with true language. See **Higher-order consciousness.**

Lateral geniculate nucleus. A specific thalamic nucleus that receives input from the optic nerve and sends projections to the primary visual cortical area, V1.

Lexicon. A collection of tokens or words in the memory of a semantically equipped or linguistic animal.

Linguistics. The study of language—that is, of phonology, semantics, and syntax. Neurolinguistics examines the brain bases of true language.

Locus coeruleus. The slightly blue neuronal nuclei in the midbrain whose diffuse ascending projections to the thalamus and cortex release noradrenaline. It is a value system important in detection of salient signals and in sleep.

Logical atomism. The notion proposed by Bertrand Russell and Ludwig Wittgenstein that minds can be constructed out of sensations and images and that, by constructing everything from simpler entities, we will have a complete description of what is the case. Wittgenstein decisively rejected this notion in his later life.

Long-term memory. Memory system with durations longer than working or short-term memory. **Episodic memory** is an example.

Machine. A device constructed of parts to perform a defined function. The most general example, perhaps, is a **Turing machine.**

Magnetoencephalography (MEG). The use of superconducting quantum interference devices (SQUIDS) to measure minute magnetic fields in the living brain. The devices used have multiple electrodes covering the entire brain and are very sensitive to temporal changes in internal currents arising from as few as twenty thousand neurons. Resolution in space is on the order of 1–1.5 centimeters, as compared with fMRI, which can get down to 3–4 millimeters or less but lacks the temporal resolution of MEG.

Maps. Maps in the brain are either topographic or nontopographic, meaning that they either do or do not conserve the geometrical relationships of their neighboring parts. In the first case, the term refers to projections from several cells in a neighborhood to another neighborhood—point to area or area to area. A key example is provided by the retinal maps in the thalamus, which map in turn to cortical area V1. Reentry among maps having different functions binds them into dynamic integrated structures.

Meaning. In neurobiology, the realization of a value system's bias or of a goal. In language, the denotation and connotation of a word—its semantics.

Memory. Term used for a variety of systems in the brain with different characteristics. In all cases, however, it implies the ability to reinvoke or repeat a specific mental image or a physical act. It is a system property that depends on changes in synaptic strengths.

Mental images. The creation by the brain of images, without external stimulation by original objects. Mental rotation is the ability consciously to turn a mental image to a new orientation.

Mental representations. A term used by some cognitive psychologists who have a computational view of the mind. The term is applied to precise symbolic constructs or codes corresponding to objects and, by their computation, putatively explaining behavior.

Metaphor. Figure of speech in which a term is used to designate an object it does not ordinarily refer to; "the evening of life" is a dictionary example. The brain origin of metaphorical reference may relate to **embodiment.**

Metastable. Stable in the complete absence of perturbation, a state typically realizable for only a short period of time but with definite structure while it lasts.

Millisecond. One thousandth of a second. Synapses function in the range of one to ten milliseconds.

Mime. Gestural communication without syntax or arbitrary symbolism.

Mind. The totality of all conscious and underlying unconscious processes originating in the brain and directing all behavior. In the philosophical sense, it is one part of the seesaw known as the mind-body problem—How is it possible for brain activity to give rise to mental activity?

Modularity. The doctrine that the brain functions largely by having different regions or modules that perform distinct functions. This view results in "localizationism," as opposed to the contrary view of "holism"—that the whole brain is required. Both views disappear when considered in terms of **selectionism** and complexity theory.

Modulation. Adjustment, adaptation, and regulation can each give rise to modulation. In electronics, variation of the amplitude, frequency, or phase of a signal.

Motor regions. A variety of cortical areas—including the primary motor cortex, premotor areas, frontal eye fields—that can give rise to muscle contractions when simulated.

Mutual information. In statistical information theory, the mutual change in **entropy** upon interaction of any two parts of a system.

Natural selection. Chief among the theories of evolution formulated by Darwin. Effectively, the idea that competition among variants in a population leads to differential reproduction, with concomitant changes in gene frequency.

Neural correlate of consciousness. Nerve activity that is functionally correlated with conscious states.

Neural Darwinism. A term applied to the **TNGS** to emphasize the application of selectionism and population thinking to the brain.

Neuromodulator. One of the substances that alter synaptic action, including a variety of neurally active peptides that can cause inhibition or excitation when applied to target neurons. There is a very large number of these substances, and they can affect pain, emotions, endocrine responses, and responses to stress.

Neuron. A nerve cell of the central or the peripheral nervous system.

Neuronal group. A tightly interactive local collection of neurons (hundreds to thousands), both excitatory and inhibitory. It is the unit of selection in the **TNGS.**

Neurophysiology. The study of the detailed electrical (and associated chemical) responses of neurons, singly or in whole systems. The experiments in this field range from tissue culture of neuronal cells to slices of the brain to probes with electrodes of whole neural areas in behaving animals.

Neurotransmitters. The chemicals released into the synaptic cleft from vesicles in the presynaptic neuron that then bind to receptors in the postsynaptic neuron, changing its transmembrane electrical potential or intracellular chemistry. Neurotransmitters are the chief means of communication between neurons. See **GABA** and **Glutamate.**

Noise. Used in electronics and information theory to refer to random or uncorrelated perturbations on a signal.

Nonconscious. Refers to brain activities unable to become conscious, in contradistinction to the **Freudian unconscious.**

Nonself. Refers to all signals not transmitted directly by the body: signals from the environment.

Nuclei. Closely connected collections of neurons with similar activities, functions, neurotransmitters, and input-output relations that have a definite neuroanatomical boundary.

Optic nerve. The main set of fibers coming from the ganglion cells of the retina and projecting to the **lateral geniculate nucleus.**

Output nuclei of the basal ganglia. The internal segment of the globus pallidus and the pars reticulata of the substantia nigra, projecting to the thalamus.

Parkinson's disease. A motor-system disease resulting from a loss of dopaminergic neurons of the substantia nigra. It is characterized by tremors, muscular rigidity, altered gait, and also occasionally by cognitive impairment.

Perceptual categorization. The process by which the brain "carves the world up" to yield adaptive categories. The most fundamental of early cognitive functions.

Perfect crystal. A crystal without any irregularities in its internal order. The third law of thermodynamics states that the entropy of a perfect crystal of a pure substance at zero degrees absolute is zero.

Phenomenal experience. The experience of **qualia;** consciousness.

Phenomenal transform. A term used here to designate

the process by which neural activity in the reentrant dynamic core (C′) entails the phenomenal property of consciousness (C).

Phonetics. The study of the sounds of speech. It is included in phonology, which also includes phonemics, the study of the smallest units of speech.

Phrenology. A discredited system of assignment of higher faculties to modules or particular regions of the brain diagnosable by bumps on the head. Founded by Joseph Gall.

Piagetian notion of self. After Jean Piaget, a noted developmental psychologist. Applied here to the stage at which a child can differentiate his or her own motor acts from motions imposed from without.

Population thinking. Darwin's seminal notion that species arise "from the bottom up" by selection of variant individuals in a population.

Postsynaptic neuron. Neuron whose properties are changed after release of neurotransmitter by presynaptic neurons.

Power. Refers to the calculated energy distribution after Fourier analysis of waveforms such as those studied by magnetoencephalography. It is the square of the **intensity.**

Premotor regions. Areas of the cortex that prepare the motor systems for movement. Another such area is the supplementary motor area, which aids in programming sequences of motor acts.

Presynaptic neuron. The neuron that releases neurotransmitters into synaptic clefts after an action potential arrives at the synapse.

Primary consciousness. The fundamental consciousness, which is proposed to arise first from reentry between regions carrying out perceptual categorization and those mediating value-category memory. Results in the creation of a scene in the remembered present. See **Higher-order consciousness.**

Privacy. The fact that consciousness is experienced as a first-person event that is not fully capable of being shared.

Procedural memory. A form of memory concerned with sequences of action or particular movements, such as bicycle riding. It is separate from episodic and semantic memory.

Process. A series of changes. William James emphasized that consciousness is a process, not a thing.

Progenitor cells. Cells in the brain capable of giving rise to neurons. They are seen in olfactory regions and in the hippocampal region of adults.

Propositional attitudes. A philosopher's term for beliefs, desires, and intentions.

Proprioceptive. Providing information about the relative positions of the body in space and the relation of the body segments to each other.

Prosopagnosia. The inability to recognize a face, even a previously familiar face, following cerebral damage. Recognition of other objects is not necessarily affected.

Protosyntax. Movement sequences and basal ganglion responses that have ordered structures like syntax.

Putamen. A nucleus of the basal ganglia.

Quale; qualia. Terms used to refer to the "feel" of consciousness experience—"what it is like to be x," where x, for example, is a human or a bat. I use the term "qualia" as coextensive with conscious experience. Consciousness reflects the integration among vast numbers of qualia. Qualia are discriminations made possible by the activity of the reentrant dynamic core.

Qualia space. A construct reflecting the fact that qualia cannot be completely isolated but exist together in a multidimensional or **high-dimensional space.**

Raphé nucleus. A collection of cell groups in the midline of the brainstem projecting to forebrain structures and releasing serotonin. A value system.

Recategorical. The process by which memory as a system property interprets current input based on past experience—that is, it does not replicate an original experience exactly.

Receptors. Proteins on the surfaces of cells that bind various chemical ligands including, for example, neurotransmitters, neuromodulators, hormones, and drugs.

Reciprocal fibers. Axonal bundles connecting two regions of the brain in both directions. These provide the anatomical basis for reentry.

Reentry. The dynamic ongoing process of recursive signaling across massively parallel reciprocal fibers connecting maps. This process results in binding and is the basis for the emergence of consciousness through the workings of the dynamic core. Allows coherent and synchronous events to emerge in the brain; that is, it is the basis for spatiotemporal correlation.

Reflex. Automatic sensorimotor loops; these are seen clearly, for example, in motor responses mediated by the spinal cord. They are nonconscious, and can be developed in the higher brain by conditioning.

Remembered present. A phrase used to describe the temporal aspect of the scene constructed in primary consciousness, suggesting the role of memory processes in that construction. Close to the **specious present** quoted by William James in *The Principles of Psychology*.

Repertoire. A set of variants in a selectional system.

Representations. Results of conscious discriminations and classifications; does not imply that the underlying neural states are representations.

Res cogitans. Descartes' term for "thinking substance," inaccessible to physical investigation. One component of substance dualism.

Res extensa. Extended things—the other end of substance dualism—one accessible to physics.

Reticular nucleus. A structure surrounding the thalamus that is also part of it, consisting mainly of inhibitory connections to specific thalamic nuclei.

Retina. The thin layer of photoreceptor cells, rods, and cones as well as ganglion cells in the eye that direct signals to the optic nerve. Along with olfactory epithelia, this is the part of the brain closest to the surface of the body.

Scene. The integration of inputs in a discriminatory fashion in primary consciousness.

Schizophrenia. Psychotic disease showing deep disorders of cognitive function, confusion, and splitting of thought and emotions. Not yet proven to be due to a specific defect of brain function but certainly a disease of consciousness.

Selectionism. The notion that biological systems operate by selection from populations of variants under a variety of constraints. The opposite of **instructionism.**

Self. A term used to refer to the genetic and immunological identity of an individual, but more to the point of this book it refers to characteristic inputs from an individual body related to its history and value systems. In its most developed form, seen with **higher-order consciousness,** it is a social self related to interactions within a speech community.

Semantic memory. Memory related to identification of objects, persons, places, and circumstances. Not episodic, however.

Semantics. The linguistic study of meaning and reference.

Sensorimotor loops. Connections between input signals and motor activities such as are seen in **global mapping.**

Sensory receptors. Specialized neurons for various modalities such as sight (rods, cones), hearing (hair cells), smell (odorant receptors), and so on.

Short-term memory. An example is the memory for telephone numbers, generally considered to be limited to seven digits, plus or minus two.

Situatedness. Presence in an environment or econiche and awareness of it.

Sleep; REM sleep. The change of state characterized by distinct changes in EEG, isolation of the brain from external input, and blockade of motor output. In rapid eye movement (REM) sleep, there is an EEG pattern of low amplitude, aperiodic fast spikes, and also dreaming. A form of consciousness occurs in REM sleep.

Somatoparaphrenia. Failure to correctly identify body parts as one's own.

Spatiotemporal correlation. According to the **TNGS,** in the absence of logic such as governs a computer, the brain must correlate time and space and sequence. It does this through **reentry.**

Specific thalamic nuclei. Nuclei of the thalamus receiving sensory signals for different modalities (see **Lateral geniculate nucleus,** for example) or signals for motor control such as those from the basal ganglia. Specific nuclei do not connect to each other but project to the cortex.

Specious present. The term quoted by William James in *The Principles of Psychology* and used to designate the present that we are aware of experiencing. See **Remembered present.**

Speech community. A group of individuals communicating over time via a particular language.

Stochastic. Subject to random processes or noise.

Striatum. The input region of the basal ganglia consisting of the caudate nucleus and the putamen.

Subcortical. Refers to structures lying below the neocortex, such as the basal ganglia, the hippocampus, and the cerebellum, among others.

Subjectivity. Refers to the private self, and collectively the first-person experiences of such a self.

Substance P. A **neuromodulator** that can activate pain receptors.

Substantia nigra. One of the basal ganglion nuclei containing cells expressing the neurotransmitter dopamine.

Subthalamic nucleus. Part of the basal ganglia. Lesions of this nucleus cause uncontrollable movements called ballismus.

Supervenient. A philosophical term to describe the relation between C′ and C meaning roughly "dependent on." A change in mental state therefore would necessarily require a change in neural state.

Supralaryngeal space. The space in the throat resulting from developmental descent of the larynx in humans and allowing a great expansion and refinement of speech sounds.

Synapse. The critical connecting structure between neurons, which mediates their signaling by electrochemical means (see **Neurotransmitters; Postsynaptic neuron; Presynaptic neuron**).

Synaptic strength. The degree by which neurotransmitter release affects postsynaptic response. Synaptic strength modification is a change in a synapse that weakens it or strengthens it, altering communication between neurons necessary for the establishment of memory. Changes of this kind reflect neural plasticity.

Synaptic vesicles. Membraneous structures containing neurotransmitters at the axonal terminals of presynaptic neurons.

Synchrony. Simultaneity of events, such as simultaneous firing among neurons.

Syntax. The study of grammar and ordering in linguistics.

Thalamus. The chief sensorimotor relay structure to the cortex. It is a key part of the thalamocortical system and the dynamic core. Consists of specific **nuclei, intralaminar nuclei,** and the **reticular nucleus.**

Third-person experience. The position of an external observer unable to directly experience another's first-person subjectivity.

TNGS. The theory of neuronal group selection, which consists of three tenets: (1) **Developmental selection** and (2) **Experiential selection,** both of which operate on repertoires of neural variants, and (3) **Reentry,** a key process assuring spatiotemporal correlation and conscious integration. It is a global brain theory explaining diversity and integration in the central nervous system.

Token. A semantic element or word in a lexicon.

Turing machine. A finite-state automaton capable of reading, writing, and erasing zeros and ones from an endless tape and then moving one space to the right or left under control of a program. Turing machines are theoretical constructs, and a theorem by Alan Turing showed that a universal Turing machine could carry out any computation based on effective procedures or algorithms.

Unconscious. The state of being unaware. See also **Nonconscious** and **Freudian unconscious.**

Unitary. The all-of-a-piece nature of a conscious scene, which cannot voluntarily be broken up into separate parts.

V1, V2, V3, V4, V5. The various areas of the striate and extrastriate regions of the cortex subserving vision.

Value; value systems. The constraining elements in a selectional system consisting in the brain of diffuse ascending systems such as the dopaminergic system, the cholinergic system, and the noradrenergic system of the **locus coeruleus.** Value systems also include the hypothalamus, the reticular activation system, and the nuclei around the periaquaductal gray matter of the brainstem. In humans, value is modifiable under some constraints.

Value-category memory. According to the extended TNGS, this memory system involves fast synaptic change leading to categories and it is altered by modulation originating in value systems. Reentrant interactions of value-category memory with systems of perceptual categorization lead to **primary consciousness.**

Variability. Refers to changes in brain responses at all levels, providing a basis for neuronal group selection.

Veridical. Matching physical reality as tested by scientific theory and measurement.

Wernicke's area. The posterior part of the superior temporal gyrus (area twenty-two), which, when damaged, can lead to the inability to produce meaningful speech or comprehend it—a condition called Wernicke's aphasia. See also **Broca's area.**

Zombie. A hypothetical humanlike creature that lacks consciousness but which, it is erroneously assumed, can carry out all of the functions of a conscious human.

Bibliographic Note

As I mentioned in the Preface, I have deliberately avoided specific references within the body of the text. A brief list of references to orient the reader may nonetheless be useful here.

For descriptive insight, nothing beats the efforts of William James:

James, W. *The Principles of Psychology*. Cambridge: Harvard University Press, 1981.

James, W. "Does Consciousness Exist?" In *Writings of William James,* edited by J. J. McDermott. Chicago: University of Chicago Press, 1977, pp. 169–183.

An excellent perspective from a more modern standpoint may be found in:

Searle, J. R. *The Mystery of Consciousness*. New York: New York Review of Books, 1997.

This publication collects Searle's reviews of various books in the field and at the same time nicely captures the salient issues. The issue of privacy is captured well by another philosopher:

Nagel, T. *Mortal Questions.* New York: Cambridge University Press, 1979.

For a different approach to similar issues, see:

Kim, J. *Mind in a Physical World.* Cambridge: MIT Press, 1998.

For a psychological theory concerned with conscious access, see:

Baars, B. J. *A Cognitive Theory of Consciousness.* Cambridge, England: Cambridge University Press, 1988.

My own efforts to build a scientific theory range over more than two decades. They are described in a series of books and papers that contain extensive bibliographies composed with scholarly attributions in mind:

Edelman, G. M., and Mountcastle, V. B. *The Mindful Brain: Cortical Organization and the Group-Selective Theory of Higher Brain Function.* Cambridge: MIT Press, 1978.
Edelman, G. M. *Neural Darwinism: The Theory of Neuronal Group Selection.* New York: Basic Books, 1987.
Edelman, G. M. *The Remembered Present: A Biological Theory of Consciousness.* New York: Basic Books, 1989.
Edelman, G. M. *Bright Air, Brilliant Fire: On the Matter of the Mind.* New York: Basic Books, 1992.

Edelman, G. M. "Neural Darwinism: The Theory of Neuronal Group Selection." *Neuron* 10 (1993): 115–125.

Edelman, G. M., and Tononi, G. *A Universe of Consciousness: How Matter Becomes Imagination.* New York: Basic Books, 2000.

For an account of the concept of degeneracy, see:

Edelman, G. M., and Gally, J. A. "Degeneracy and Complexity in Biological Systems." *Proceedings of the National Academy of Sciences USA* 98 (2001): 13763–13768

For two recent papers considering various aspects of a scientifically based approach, see:

Crick, F., and Koch, C. "A Framework for Consciousness." *Nature Neuroscience* 6 (2003): 119–126.

Edelman, G. M. "Naturalizing Consciousness: A Theoretical Framework." *Proceedings of the National Academy of Sciences USA* 100 (2003): 5520–5524.

This last paper succinctly puts forth the views elaborated in this book. For related references to neural correlates of consciousness, the following volume is an excellent source:

Metzinger, T., editor. *Neural Correlates of Consciousness: Empirical and Conceptual Questions.* Cambridge: MIT Press, 2000.

For works bearing on the experiments described in Chapter 9, see:

Leopold, D. A., and Logothetis, N. "Activity Changes in Early Visual Cortex Reflect Monkey's Percepts During Binocular Rivalry." *Nature* 379 (1996): 549–553.

Tononi, G., Srinivasan, R., Russell, D. P., and Edelman, G. M. "Investigating Neural Correlates of Conscious Perception by Frequency-Tagged Neuromagnetic Responses." *Proceedings of the National Academy of Sciences USA* 95 (1998): 3198–3203.

Srinivasan, R., Russell, D. P., Edelman, G. M., and Tononi, G. "Increased Synchronization of Neuromagnetic Responses During Conscious Perception." *Journal of Neuroscience* 19 (1999): 5435–5448.

Finally, a set of accounts with which I disagree should be included for balance and fairness. The modern authors listed below find themselves in the distinguished company of René Descartes.

Descartes, R. *The Philosophical Works of Descartes,* 2 vols., edited by E. Haldane and G. Ross. Cambridge, England: Cambridge University Press, 1975.

Popper, K., and Eccles, J. F. *The Self and Its Brain.* New York: Springer, 1977.

Penrose, R. *Shadows of the Mind: A Search for the Missing Science of Consciousness.* New York: Oxford University Press, 1994.

McGinn, C. *The Problem of Consciousness: Essays Toward a Resolution.* Oxford: Blackwell, 1996.

Chalmers, D. *The Conscious Mind: In Search of a Fundamental Theory.* New York: Oxford University Press, 1996.

If an insatiable reader wishes an even longer list of references, I refer him or her to David Chalmers's annotated compendium on the World Wide Web:

http://www.u.arizona.edu/~chalmers/biblio.html

The exploding list of references speaks to the conclusion that the understanding of consciousness has a promising scientific future.

Index

acetylcholine, and cholinergic nuclei, 25, 152

action potential, 18, 149

adaptive immune system, 131–132, 149

algorithms, and computation, 38, 111, 153

alien hand syndrome, 136

amino-acid sequences, and genetic code, 43, 160

amplification, and selectionism, 42

amygdala, 26

animals: and higher-order consciousness, 134, 161–162; and phenomenal transform, 81; primary consciousness of, 11, 56, 57–58, 59, 77, 97, 134

anosognosia, 38, 136, 143, 149, 153

anterior commissure, and disconnection syndromes, 143

aphasia, 100, 149, 180

ascending systems. *See* value systems

association areas, 89, 150

associativity, 150; and conscious experience, 135–136; and degenerate interactions, 114, 126; and language acquisition, 103, 136

atomism, logical, 107

attention, 150; and basal ganglia circuitry, 88, 90, 94, 95, 127, 143; and concious states, 7, 94–95, 143; motor components, 95; and nonconscious execution, 88, 93–94; and TNGS, 127–128. *See also* focal attention

auditory discrimination, 102

automaticity, 88, 127–128, 144–145, 150
automatic motor processes, 93, 144
autonomic nervous system, 57, 73, 128–129, 133, 150
axons, and synaptic connections, 17, 18, 150

basal ganglia, 16, 21, 53, 88–89, 150, 170; and attentional states, 143; and automaticity, 127–128; motor circuitry of, 88–96; motor sequencing and control, 24, 103; polysynaptic loop structure of, 24, 26–28, 96, 163; and surround effects, 126; thalamocortical system and, 69, 70–71
binding problem, 36, 44, 150–151
binocular rivalry, 108, 110, 151
bipedal posture, 102, 103, 151
blindsight, 143, 151
blind spot, and brain dynamics, 37, 136
brachiation, and gestural communication, 102
brain: anatomy and dynamics of, 14–23, 26, 27, 151; and ascending value systems, 25–26, 28; capacity to generalize, 38; computer model of, 28–30, 33, 35–36, 39, 45–46, 114; and integration, 136; motor functions, 23–24; as origin of consciousness, 4–5, 6–7, 21; sensory and cognitive functioning of, 14–23
brain scans, 151. *See also* magnetoencephalography (MEG)
brainstem, 16, 151; and categorization, 72–73; and modulation of emotion, 133
Brentano, Franz, 125, 164
Broca's area, of cerebral cortex, 99–100, 101, 151–152
Bruner, Jerome, 100

C, as conscious process, 78–86, 130, 152; and attention, 127–128; and integration, 121; relationship with C′ (neural activity), 115–116, 117, 122–123, 145–146; socially defined self and, 137–138
C′, as neural activity, 78–86, 130, 152; and attention, 127–128; centrality of, to complex subjective states, 130; and looped reentrant interactions, 122–123; relation-

ship with C (conscious process), 115–116, 117, 122–123, 145–146; and socially defined self, 137–138
categorization. *See* perceptual categorization
caudate nucleus, 89
causal efficacy, 75, 86, 152
causality, and conscious process, 76–78, 81–82, 152
cell body, 17, 152
cell migration, 28–29, 152
cerebellum, 16, 21, 96, 152; and automaticity, 128; circuitry of, 89, 95; motor control and sequencing, 23, 88, 89; and temporal succession, 53, 88
cerebral cortex, 15–17, 83, 152, 154; and basal ganglia, 89–92; development and evolution of, 102; hemispheres, 20, 154; and memory, 51, 88; motor areas of, 91, 92, 93; and thalamocortical system, 26–28, 54, 69, 70, 71, 88–89. *See also* somatosensory cortex; Wernicke's area, of cerebral cortex
channel, 17–19, 152
cholinergic nuclei, 25, 93, 133, 152

closure (filling-in), and brain dynamics, 120, 136, 153
coarticulated sounds, 102, 153
codons (triplets), and genetic code, 43, 160
cognitive defects, and basal ganglia, 93
cognitive science, and "representation," 103–105, 111
coherency, and reentry, 45, 153
color experiences, and qualia, 64–65
complex systems, and integration, 65–68, 153
computations, 105, 153
computer models, 41, 153; of brain and mind, 28–30, 33, 35–36, 39, 45, 107, 114; and conscious process, 85–86
concepts, 153–154; formation of, 50, 53; and mapping of universals, 104–105
consciousness: of consciousness, 101, 116; and discrimination, 10, 72–73, 141–142; experience of, 4–13; and integration, 7–8, 136; neural correlates of, 107–112, 118; perceptual categorization and, 72–73; and self-awareness, 73, 116; structure

consciousness (continued)
and dynamics of, and
TNGS, 141–145. *See also* C,
as conscious process; C', as
neural activity; higher-order
consciousness; primary consciousness
conscious state, and TNGS:
general properties of, 119–
125; informational func-
tions, 119, 120, 125–128;
and irreducibility, 124–125;
subjective properties, 119,
120, 128–130; summary
and testability of, 110, 113–
118
corpus callosum, 20, 143, 154
cortex. *See* cerebral cortex
corticocortical tracts, 20
corticostriatal projections, 92,
154
corticothalamic projections, 20

Darwin, Charles, 1–3; *The Descent of Man,* 2; and natural
selection, 32–33, 47, 157
Darwinism, neural, 33, 147.
See also neuronal group selection, theory of (TNGS)
degeneracy, 43–46, 154; and
dynamic core, 70, 72, 121;
and genetic code, 160; of
neural networks, 44–45, 52,

111, 114–115, 147; re-
entrant circuitry of, 46, 106,
121, 135; selective processes,
114; and synaptic response,
51, 52
dendrites, of neurons, 17, 18,
154
Descartes, René, 2, 155–156,
174
The Descent of Man (Darwin),
2
developmental selection, and
TNGS, 39–40, 155
differentiation, of conscious experience, 31, 106, 128, 155
digital computation, and brain
action, 29–30. *See also* computer models
disconnection syndromes, 143
discrimination, 155; adaptive
value of, 135; auditory, 102;
and qualia, 70, 72, 146; and
reentrant interactions, 141–
142; and subjectivity, 131
dissociative syndromes, 143
distributed systems, 36, 41,
155
diversity, and selectional systems, 41–42
dopamine, as neurotransmitter,
24, 25, 92, 155
dopaminergic projection, from
substantia nigra, 92

dopaminergic system, 133

dualism, 137, 145, 155–156, 174

dynamic core, 156; adaptive behavior and, 132–133; and categorization, 74; and consciousness, 84–85, 96, 115, 127, 143; cortex interactions, 74, 94; as functional cluster, 69, 74, 96, 156, 159; modulation of, 127–128, 142–143; and phenomenal transform, 78–81; reentrant interactions, 69–72, 77–78, 79, 85, 96, 143

econiche, 136, 156, 176

effective procedures, and computer models, 35

embodiment, 5, 156

emotion, 156; and amygdala, 26; and self-discrimination, 129; and value systems, 130, 133

endogenous opioids, 26, 156

enkephalin, 26, 156

entailment, and relationship of C and C′, 80, 81, 85–86, 146, 156

entropy, informational, 66–67, 157

epigenetic processes, 29, 157

epiphenomenonalism, and conscious process, 82, 85, 137, 145, 157

episodic memory, 22–23, 51, 88, 157, 162

evolution, 157; and brain development, 32–33; of conscious process, 54–57, 85, 138–139; of primary consciousness, 57, 132; as selectional system, 32–33, 41; value-system constraint, 42, 138–139

evolution, theory of, 157; and biological basis of consciousness, 1–3; and TNGS, as neural Darwinism, 41–43, 157

excitatory inputs, 25, 89–90

experiential selection, and TNGS, 39, 114, 157–158. *See also* selectionism

explanatory gap, 11–12, 158

eye movements, and constructive "filling-in," 126–127

feedback, 41, 158

filling-in, as neural dynamic, 116, 120, 122, 124, 127

first-person perspective, 63, 74–75, 158

fMRI (functional magnetic resonance imaging), 151, 158, 166

focal attention, 158; and conscious state, 7, 61, 120; and dynamic core, 94–95, 127, 142–143

foveal discrimination, and eye movement, 126–127

frequency tag, 159

Freudian unconscious, 95, 159

fringe effects, and conscious state, 7, 126–127, 159

functional cluster, 69, 96, 156, 159

functional connectivity, 67, 68, 159

functional magnetic resonance imaging (fMRI), 151, 158, 166

functional segregation, 68, 159

GABA (gamma-aminobutyric acid), as neurotransmitter, 19, 24, 93, 159–160

Gall, Franz Joseph, 30, 171

genetic code, and degeneracy, 43, 160

gestalt phenomenon, 160; as feature of conscious state, 116, 120; and synchrony of reentry, 124

gestural communication, 102, 160

glia (support cells), 29, 160

global brain theory, 33. *See also* neuronal group selection, theory of (TNGS)

global mapping, 160, 176; inhibitory output of, 95, 127; and perceptual categorization, 49–50, 53, 56, 144; and TNGS, 114–115

globus pallidus, 89, 90, 92, 160–161, 170

glutamate, as neurotransmitter, 19, 92, 161, 169

glutamatergic inputs, 25, 89–90

gray matter, of brain, 16, 152

Hayek, Friedrich von, 22

Hebb, Donald, 22, 161

Hebb synapse, 22, 161

hemineglect, as neuropsychological syndrome, 136, 143, 161

Heraclitean illusion, 103, 134, 161

high-dimensional space, 135, 161. *See also* qualia space

higher-order consciousness, 8–9, 58–59, 161–162; evolution and development of, 73, 101; experiments and magnetic field testing, 107–111; linguistic ability and,

9, 58, 100, 101, 102–103, 112; and representation, 97–112; self-concepts of, 77, 129–130, 134, 137–138; TNGS theory, 116–130

hippocampus, 16, 53, 157, 162; and episodic memory, 22, 51, 88, 99; synaptic mechanisms of, 21–23

histaminergic system, 25

holistic view, of brain function, 30–31, 168

homeostatic system, 57, 133, 162

hominines, and higher-order consciousness, 58, 98, 100, 102

homologous structures, 59, 132, 162

homunculus, 46–47; and experience of conscious process, 85, 86; as observer, 74–75

Hox genes, 29, 162

Huntington's disease, 93, 162

Huxley, T. H., 82–83, 84

hypnotic trance, 143

hypothalamic systems, and emotional response, 133

hypothalamus, 25, 150, 162–163

hysteria, as dissociative syndrome, 143

ideal (perfect) gas, 66, 67, 163

identity, 131–139, 163

illusion, 163; phenomenology of, 36–37; and reentrant connections, 122, 136

imagery, and brain dynamics, 105, 126, 144

immune system, 41, 42, 44, 131, 149

individual variation, and evolution, 132

individuation, and self-discrimination, 129. *See also* self-concept

informational properties, 120, 125, 163

inhibitory loops, structure of, and basal ganglia, 24, 26–28, 96, 163

instructionism, 41, 163, 175. *See also* logic; selectionism

integration, 164; brain activity and, 31, 106, 136; and complex systems, 65–68; of conscious state, 121, 122; and higher-order consciousness, 135

intentionality, and consciousness, 105–106, 120, 125, 164

intralaminar nuclei, of thalamus, 21, 31, 89, 164

irreducibility, 124–125, 164

James, William, 4–7, 55, 82, 83–84, 134, 172, 174; "Does Consciousness Exist?" 6; *The Principles of Psychology,* 4, 82–83, 177

Jamesian properties, 7, 31, 164

Kanizsa triangle, 36–37, 163

kinesthetic response, 57, 164; and motor control, 133; and self-perception, 72–73, 129

language, 164–165; and higher-order consciousness, 58, 98, 112; origins and development of, 99–103, 135

Lashley, Karl, 34

lateral geniculate nucleus, of thalamus, 20, 165, 170

lexicon, 98–99, 103, 118, 165

linguistic ability, 165; development of, 100–103, 135–136; and higher-order consciousness, 9, 118

locus coeruleus, and ascending-value system, 25, 26–28, 133, 165

logic: as organizing principle, 41; and selectionism, 147–148

logical atomism, 165

long-term memory, 23, 88, 99, 165

magnetic resonance imaging (fMRI), 151, 158, 166

magnetoencephalography (MEG), 107–109, 110, 118, 151, 159, 164, 166

maps, 40, 41, 44–45, 49–50, 53, 100, 104, 114–115, 122, 136, 166

meaning, in neurobiology, 105, 166. *See also* semantic capabilities

memory, 50–53, 166, 176; hippocampus and, 21–22, 51, 99; as nonrepresentational, 52–53, 104–105, 115; and perceptual categorization, 114–115, 129–130; reentrant interactions, 124; sensory and motor modulation, 115, 124, 143, 144. *See also* episodic memory; long-term memory; procedural memory; short-term memory; value-category memory

mental images, 9, 104, 105, 167

mental representations, 103–107, 109, 167

metaphor, 167; and higher-order consciousness, 103, 135–136

metastable, 74, 115, 126, 167

milliseconds, and neural response, 144, 167

mime, as gestural communication, 102, 167

mind, neural basis of, 1–3, 140–148, 167

modularity, and brain function, 30–31, 167–168

modulation, 168; of dynamic core, 127, 142–143

motor control: and basal ganglia, 24, 90–93, 127; and concepts, 105; and conscious attention, 61–62, 90, 95, 144–145; global mapping, 114–115, 144; language acquisition, 102–103

motor regions, of the brain, 23–24, 88, 91, 92, 168

mutual information, 66, 163, 168

natural selection: and degeneracy, 44; and global brain theory (TNGS), 2–3, 32–33; and process of consciousness, 48; as selectional system, 41, 42

natural selection, theory of, 1–2, 47, 168

nervous systems, and natural selection, 4, 41, 42

neural correlate of consciousness, 13, 59, 107, 118, 137, 145, 168

neural Darwinism, and TNGS, 32–47, 147, 168

neural dynamics, and reentry, 116

neuroanatomy, and complex systems, 67

neuromodulators, 25–26, 168–169

neuronal groups, 169; degeneracy of, and memory, 52; and reentry dynamics, 123–124

neuronal group selection, theory of (TNGS): as global brain theory, 33–39, 45–47, 179; and memory, 50–53, 114–115; reentrant interactions, and degeneracy, 39–41, 43–45, 46, 176; tenets of, and selectionism, 39–45, 53–54, 72, 84–85, 114, 155–157, 179. *See also* conscious state, and TNGS

neurons, 14, 15, 16–19, 169

neuropeptides, 25–26, 168–169

neurophysiology, 109, 111, 169

neuropsychological syndromes, and illusory phenomena, 37–38, 143

Neurosciences Institute, 118
neurotransmitters, 17–19, 24,
    169
noise, and brain function, 35,
    114, 169
nonconscious brain activity,
    88, 93–94, 95–96, 143,
    169
nonrepresentational memory,
    52–53
nonself, 129, 170
noradrenaline, 25, 165
nuclei, as clusters of neurons,
    20, 170

obsessive-compulsive disorders,
    93
optic nerve, 20, 37, 170

parietal cortex, 17, 91, 94, 161
Parkinson's disease, 24, 92–93,
    170
pars reticulata, of substantia ni-
    gra, 90, 170
pattern recognition, 38–39,
    147. *See also* selectionism
Pax genes, 29, 162
perception: and context, 36–
    38; motor elements of, 144
perceptual categorization, 49–
    50, 117, 160, 170; and
    consciousness, 55–57,
    72–73, 114–115, 125,

143, 144; evolution of, 54,
    55, 57; and memory sys-
    tems, 50–51, 53, 55–57,
    121, 129–130; and re-
    entrant interactions, 49–50,
    54, 56, 57, 121; and TNGS,
    50–51, 114–115, 117,
    125
perfect crystal, 66, 68, 170
phenomenal experience, or con-
    sciousness, 61–63, 170
phenomenal transform, 77–78,
    117, 170–171; and neural
    core processes, 78–80, 86;
    and reentrant interactions,
    123; and self-reference, 128–
    129
phenomenology of illusions,
    36–38
phenotype, properties of, 146
phonetics, 171
phrenology, and brain faculties,
    30, 171
Piaget, Jean, 171
Piagetian notion of self, 129,
    171
polysynaptic loop structure, of
    basal ganglia, 24, 26–28, 96,
    163
population thinking, 33–35,
    171
postsynaptic neurons, 17, 18,
    20, 22, 171

prefrontal cortex, and cognitive defects, 93

premotor regions, 50, 89, 92, 171

presynaptic neurons, 17, 18, 22, 172

primary consciousness, 8–9, 48, 56–59, 77, 97, 172, 180; in animals, 63–64, 77, 97; evolutionary path of, 132, 133; links with higher-order consciousness, 59, 99, 116–118; mental images in, 105, 167; and "remembered present," 118, 134, 144; and self-concept, 77, 97, 132, 133–134; and TNGS, 116–118

primary motor cortex, 23, 154

primates, and higher-order consciousness, 98. *See also* hominines

The Principles of Psychology (James), 4, 82–83, 177

privacy, 75, 172

procedural memory, 24, 51, 150, 172

progenitor cells, 28–29, 172

propositional attitudes, 119, 172

proprioception, 57, 172; and motor control, 133; and self-systems, 73, 128–129

prosopagnosia, 143, 172–173

protosyntax, 103, 173

putamen, of basal ganglia, 89, 173

qualia: and causality, 152; and higher-order consciousness, 135; and high-order discrimination, 64–65, 85, 115, 117, 125, 142, 146; and phenomenal transform, 62–63, 77–78, 86, 117; and primary consciousness, 10–11, 73–74, 115; and representation, 106; as subjective conscious state, 3, 10–13, 120, 173

qualia space: and discriminatory capabilities, 73, 115, 128, 129; and integration, 72; and phenomenal transform, 86

raphé nucleus, 25, 133, 173

rapid eye movement (REM) sleep, and conscious states, 9–10, 122, 144, 176

recategorical memory, 52, 173

receptors, 18–20, 173, 176

reciprocal fibers, 20, 39, 173

reentrant mapping, and TNGS, 39–41, 43, 136

reentry, 110, 114, 116, 121, 141, 143, 174; concatenated loops, 122–123, 153; degeneracy of, 45–46, 106, 135; and dynamic core, 69–72, 79, 95, 121, 143; "looped" or cyclic nature of, 122–123; measurement of, and MEG, 107–109, 110, 118; and primary consciousness, 56; and spatiotemporal coordination, 41, 45, 100, 114; thalamocortical system and, 54–55, 68–72

reflex, 174

"remembered present," 8, 55, 103, 118, 134, 144, 174

repertoire, 33, 39, 40, 42, 111, 114, 174

representation, 174; and consciousness, 104–107; and MEG experiment, 107–109, 110; and reentrant patterns, 109, 111–112

repression, and Freudian unconscious, 95

res cogitans, 2, 156, 174

res extensa, 156, 175

reticular nucleus, of thalamus, 21, 54–55, 68, 94, 127, 175

retina, and eye movements, 126, 175

Russell, Bertrand, 165

scene, 7–8, 11, 48, 55–58, 61, 115, 116, 175

schizophrenia, 10, 155, 175

selectionism, 157–158, 168, 175; and global brain theory, 32–33; and relationship with logic, 147–148; and TNGS, 39, 41–43, 114

self-concept, 175; characteristics and development of, 132–134; and consciousness, 74–75, 77, 134, 175; and dynamic core, 77, 132; and higher-order consciousness, 101, 116; Piagetian notion of, 129; as process, 137–138; and self-discrimination, 128–130; and semantic capabilities, 77, 116, 118

semantic capabilities: and higher-order consciousness, 9, 58, 77, 98, 99, 116, 118; origins of, 99–102

semantic memory, 176

semantics, 166, 176

sensorimotor loops, 176. See also global mapping

sensory modalities, and cerebral cortex, 124

sensory receptors, 176

sequencing, and basal ganglia, 24

serotonin, 25

short-term memory, 51, 53, 88, 99, 176

sleep, and consciousness, 9–10, 176. *See also* rapid eye movement (REM) sleep

social development, and individuation, 116, 129–130, 137

social values, 138

somatoparaphrenia, 136, 176

somatosensory components, of "self" system, 73

somatosensory cortex, 17, 35–36, 91

spatiotemporal coordination, 41, 114

spatiotemporal correlation, 176

"specious present," 55, 177

speech community, 137, 175, 177

Sperry, Roger, 84

split-brain syndrome, 20

SQUIDS (superconducting quantum interference devices), 166

stochastic processes, 29, 177

striatum, of basal ganglia, 89, 90–92, 177

subcortical structures, 87–88, 100, 177

subcortical value systems, 68

subjectivity, 177; and conscious states, 63, 120; and self-reference, 128–130, 131, 134

substantia nigra, 89, 90, 92, 170, 177

subthalamic nucleus, 89, 90, 177

supervenience, 81–82, 178

supralaryngeal space, 102, 178

surround effects, and conscious state, 124, 126–127

synapses, 15, 16–19, 178; and developmental selection, 35, 39, 54; strength and efficacy of, 22–23, 178

synaptic response, and memory, 22, 50–52, 54

synaptic vesicles, 18, 178

synchrony, and reentrant circuits, 41, 45, 114, 124, 178

syntactic capabilities, 98, 99–103

syntax, 178

thalamic nuclei, 21, 23, 31, 54, 177

thalamocortical maps, and temporal succession, 53

thalamocortical projections, 20

thalamocortical system, 16, 26–28; and basal ganglia, 88–96; evolutionary changes in, 54; and primary consciousness, 115; reentrant dynamics of, 68–72, 95, 96

thalamus, 177, 178–179; anatomy and dynamics of, 19–21; and attentional states, 143; and basal ganglia, 88, 89, 90, 91, 170; evolutionary changes in, 54–55; intralaminar nuclei, 21, 31, 54, 179; and reentrant connections, 54; and somatosensory cortex, 23, 35–36, 55. *See also* thalamocortical system

third-person perspective, 74–75, 179

TNGS. *See* neuronal group selection, theory of (TNGS)

triplets, and amino-acid sequences, 43, 160

Turing, Alan, 179

Turing machine, 33, 84, 153, 179

unconscious, Freudian, 95

unconscious state, 9–10, 179. *See also* nonconscious brain activity

unitary scene, 7–8, 10, 61, 64–65, 68, 115, 116, 123, 128, 135, 179

value-category memory, 53–54, 117, 180; and perceptual categorization, 55–57; and primary consciousness, 56, 57, 58, 115, 180; and reentrant interactions, 56, 57, 115, 121, 180; self-discrimination and, 132–133

value systems, 25–28, 113, 180; and amplification, 42; and emotional response, 133; evolutionary selection and, 42, 113–114, 138–139; and perceptual categorization, 72–73, 125; and population thinking, 34–35; and self-discrimination, 128–129, 130. *See also* value-category memory

variability, 113–114, 180

veridical reality, 135, 136, 180

vision, and "fringe" effects, 124, 126–127

visual cortical areas (V1, V2, V3, V4, V5), 20, 30–31, 68, 124, 165, 179 visual perception, and imagery, 126

Wallace, Alfred, 1–2

Wernicke's area, of cerebral cortex, 99–100, 101, 180

Wittgenstein, Ludwig, 106, 165

zombie hypothesis, 180; and C–C′ entailment, 80, 145–146